TATTOO
COLORING BOOK

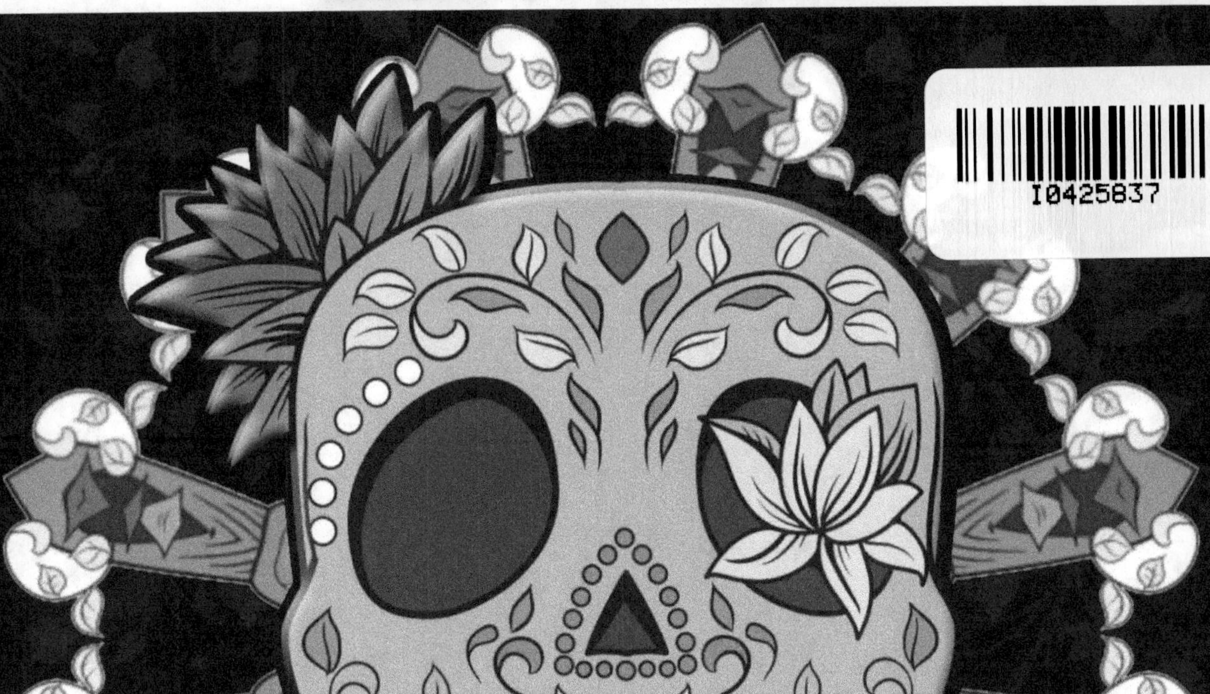

SKULL ADULT COLORING BOOKS

BLACK PAGE

COLOR TEST PAGE

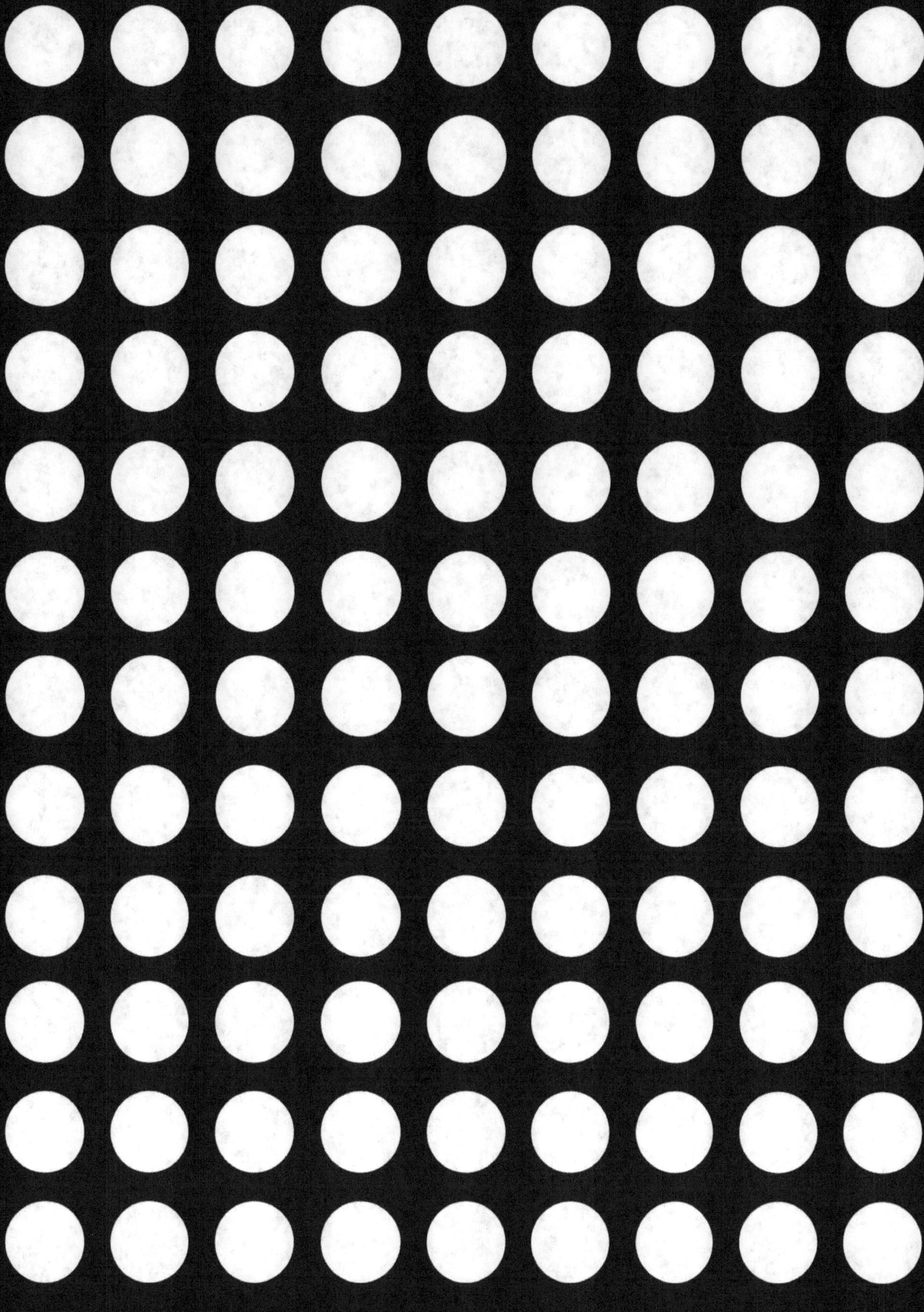

Z

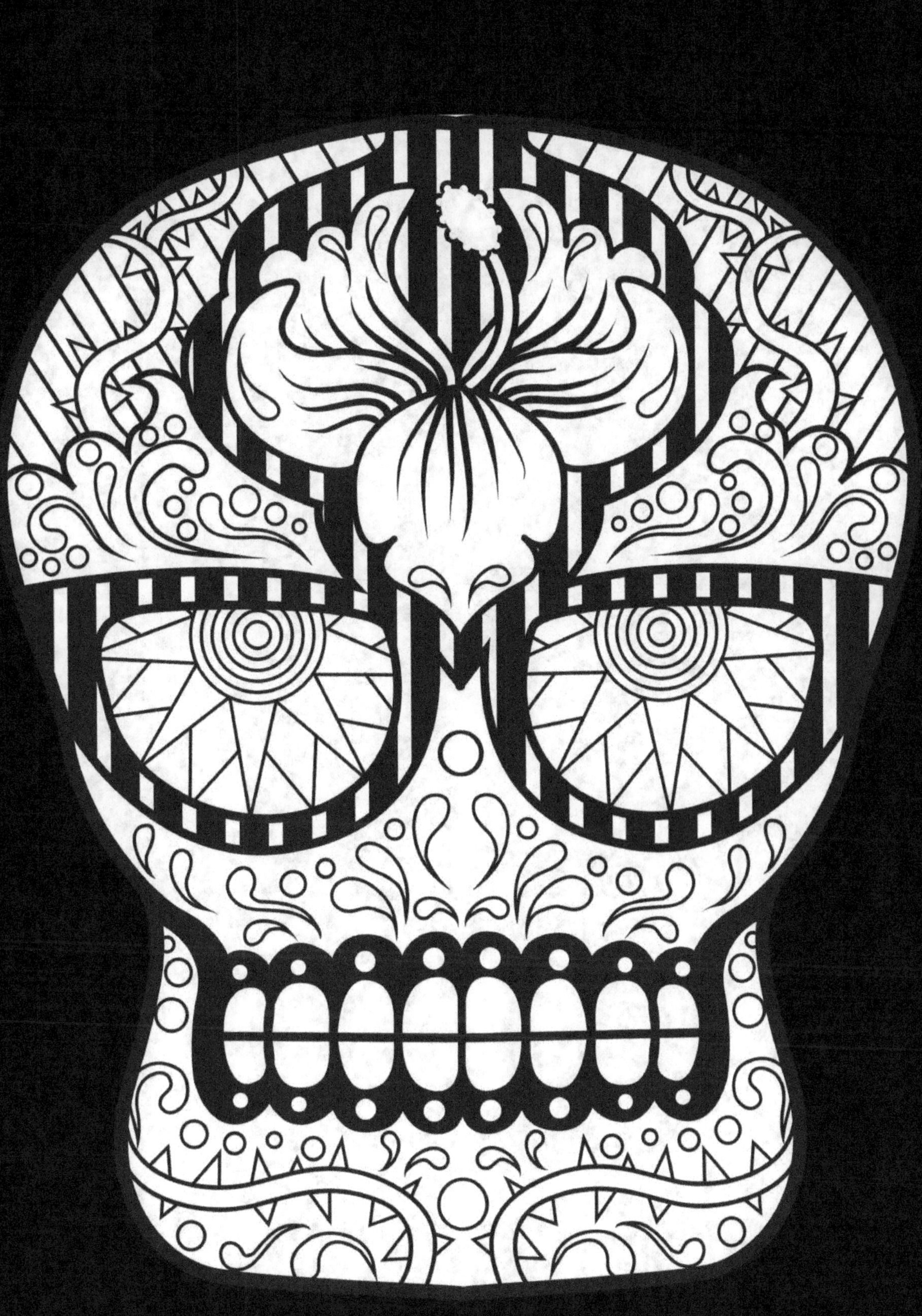

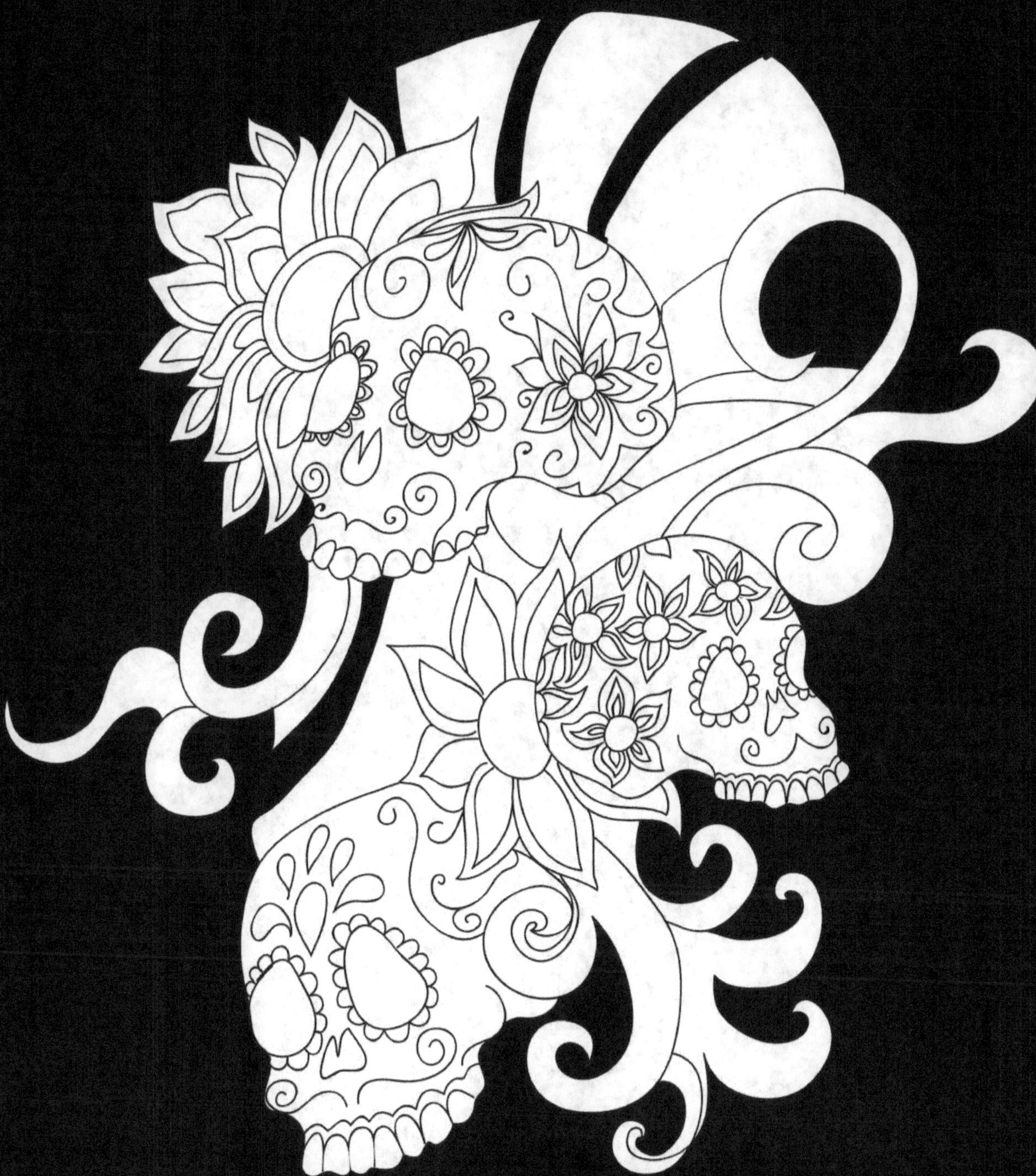

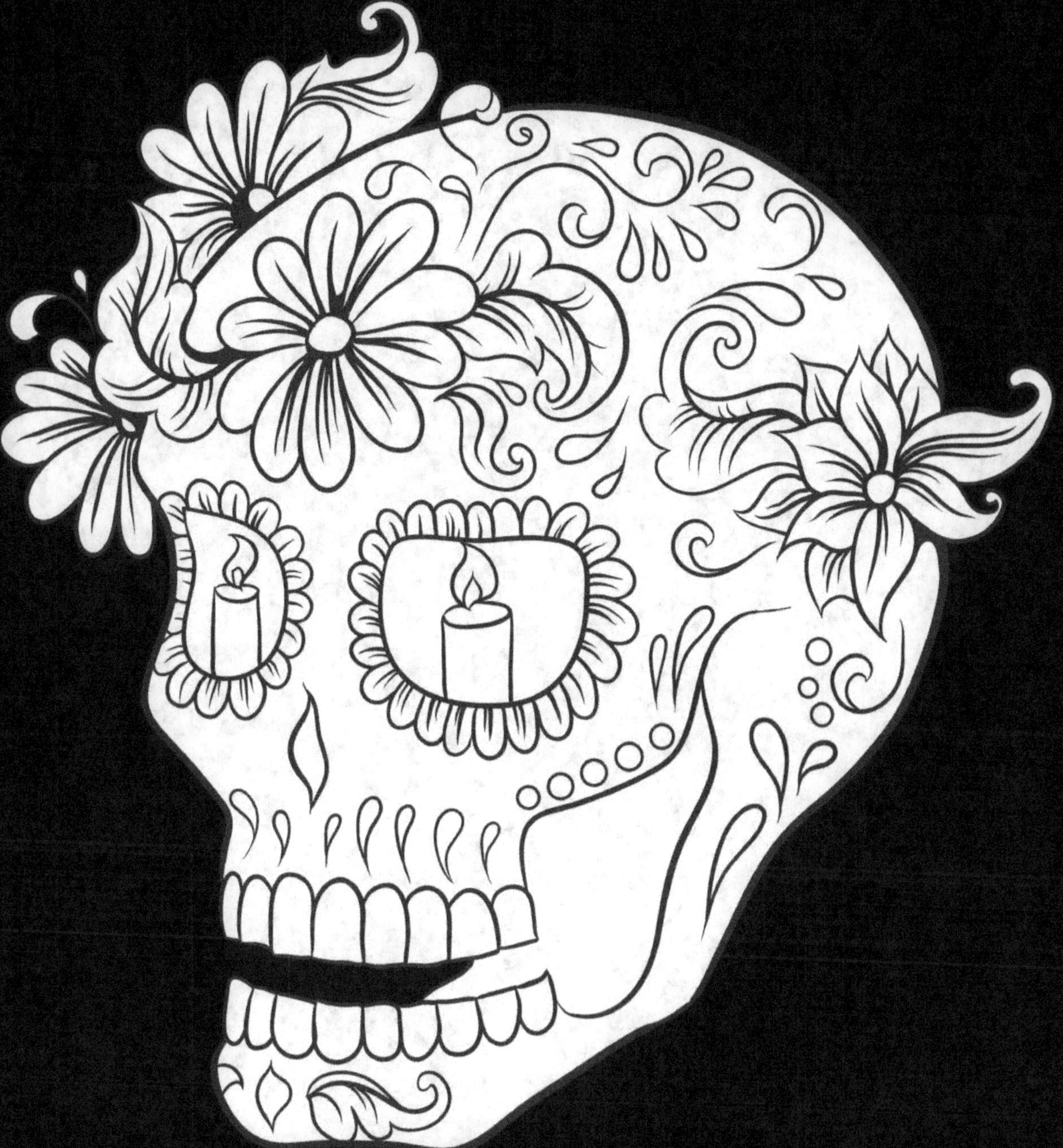

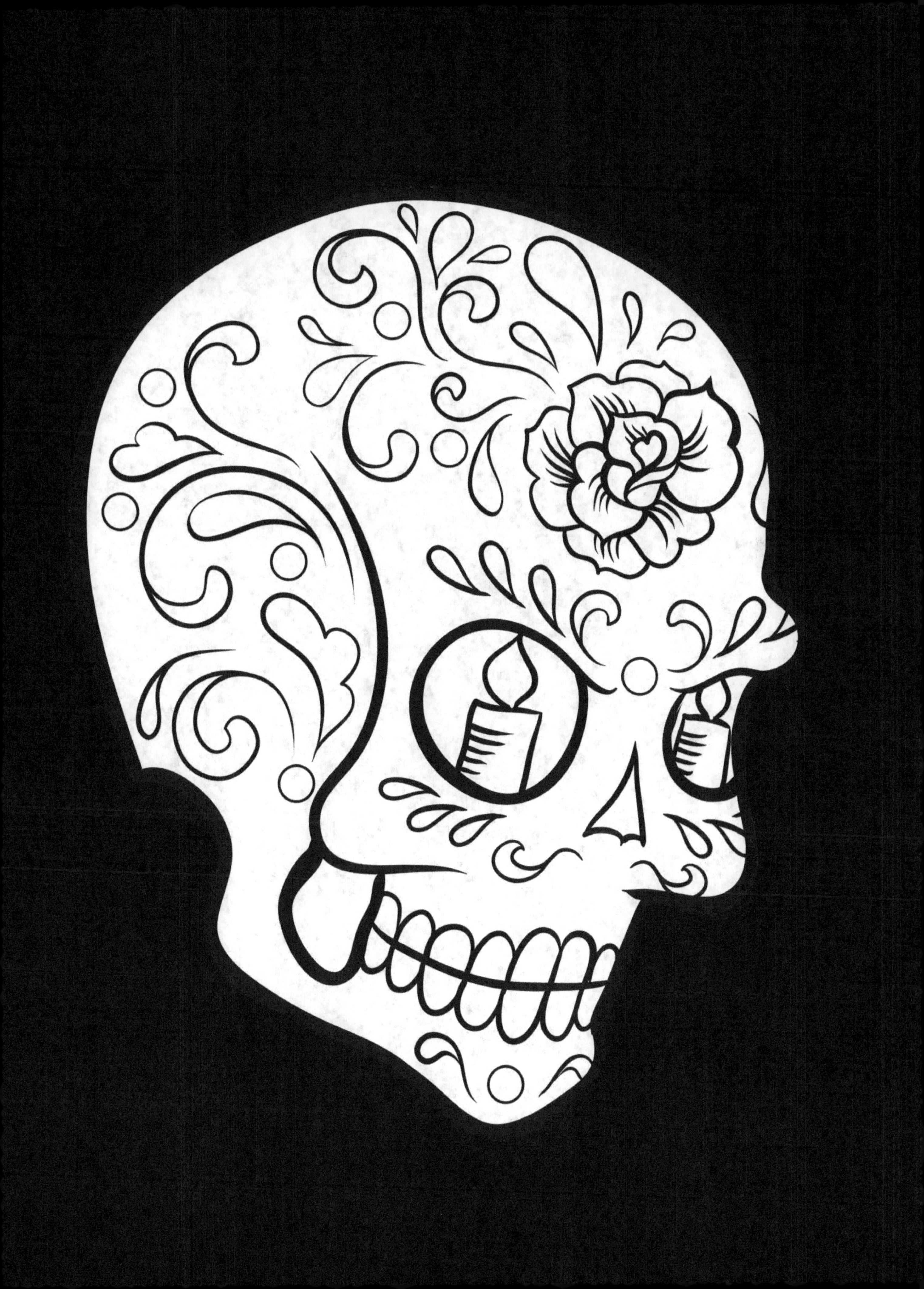

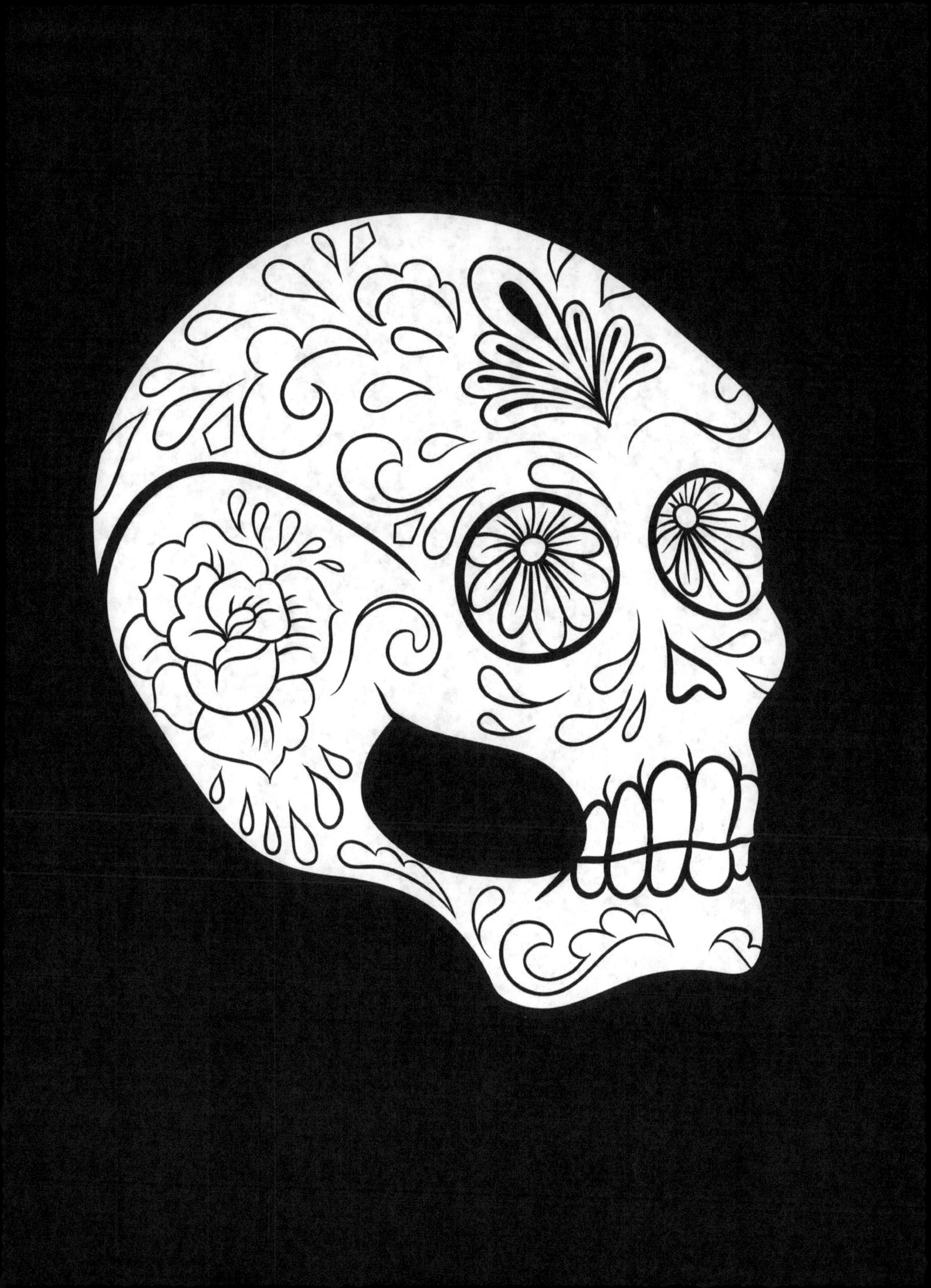

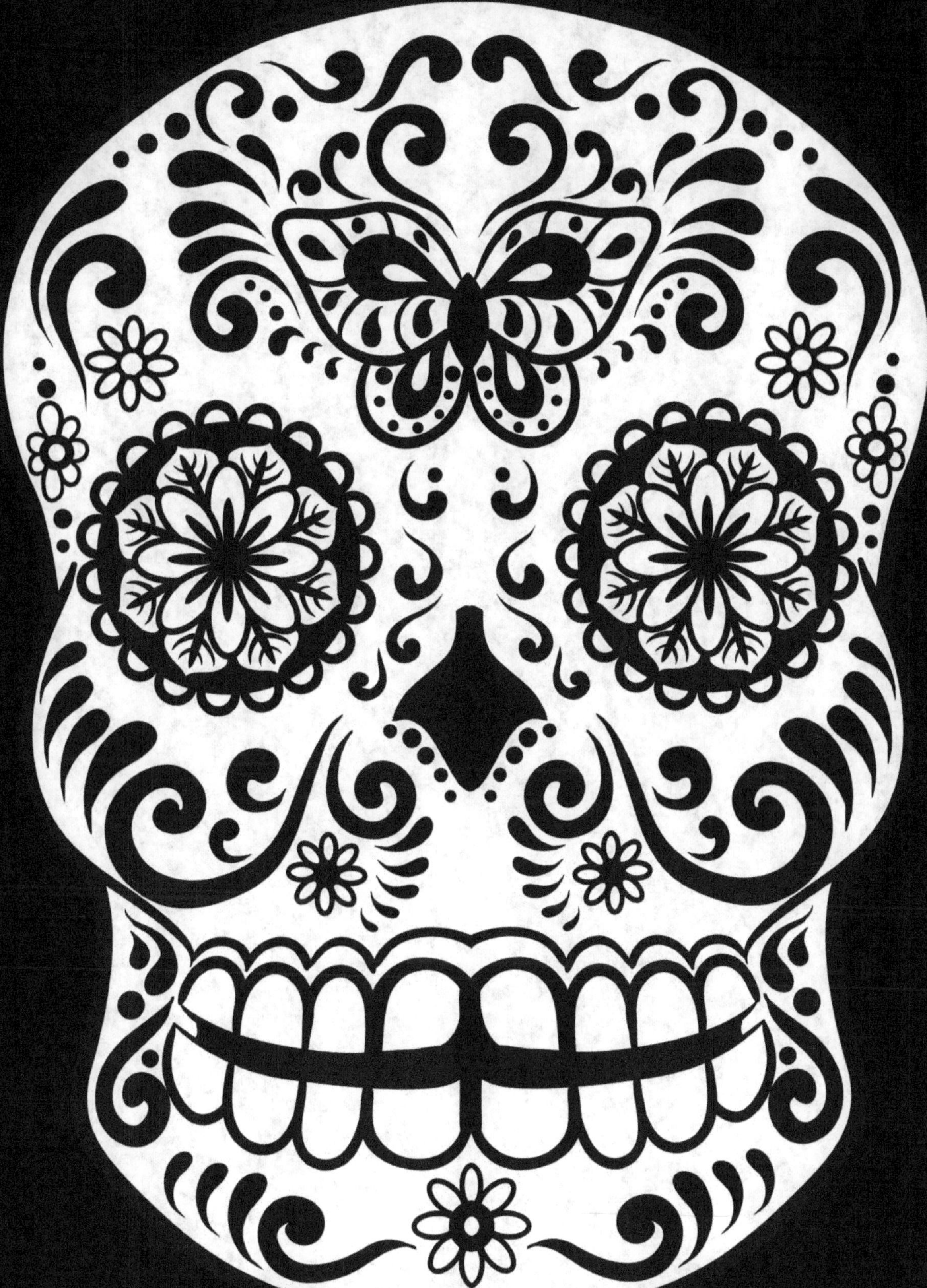

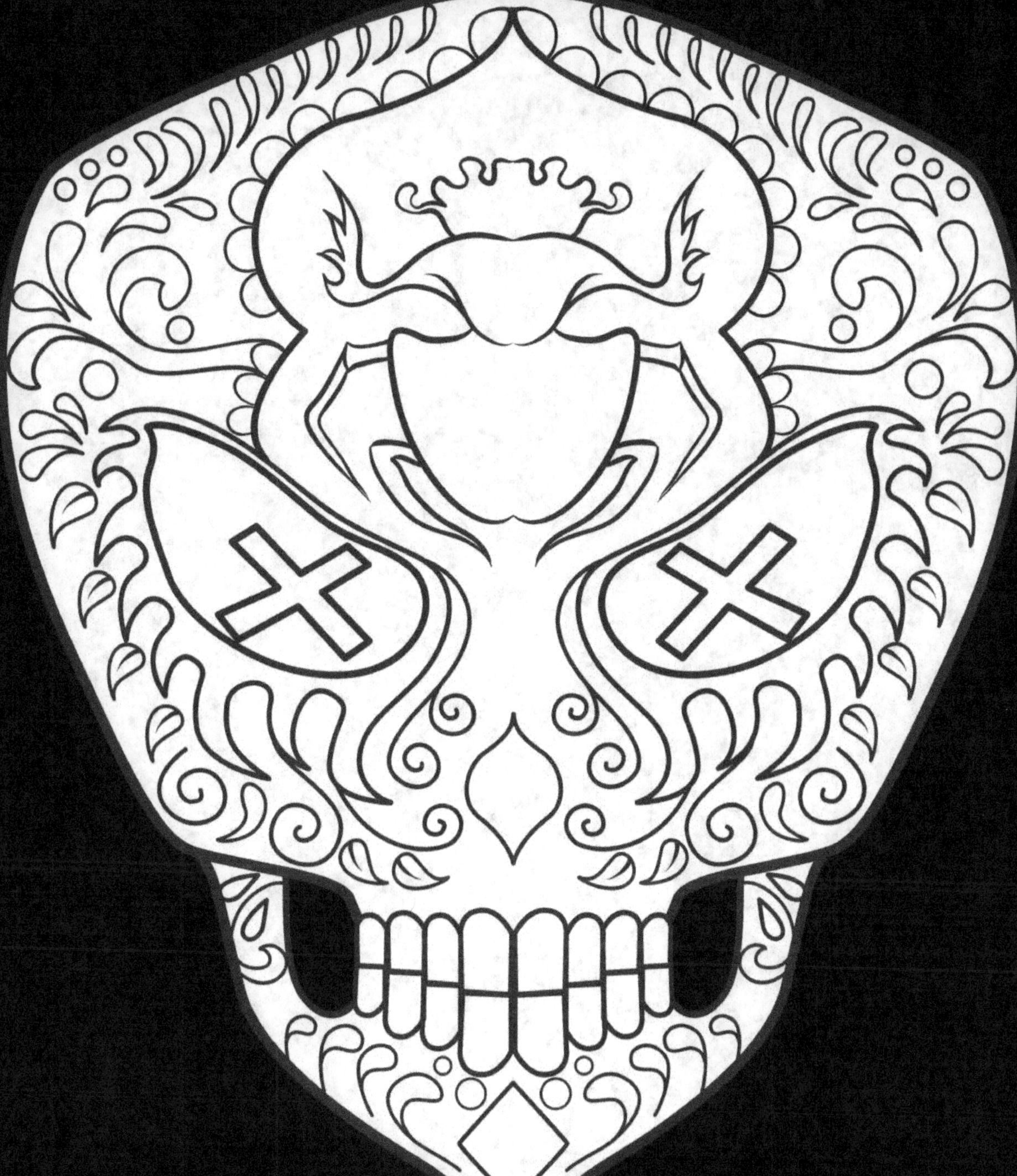

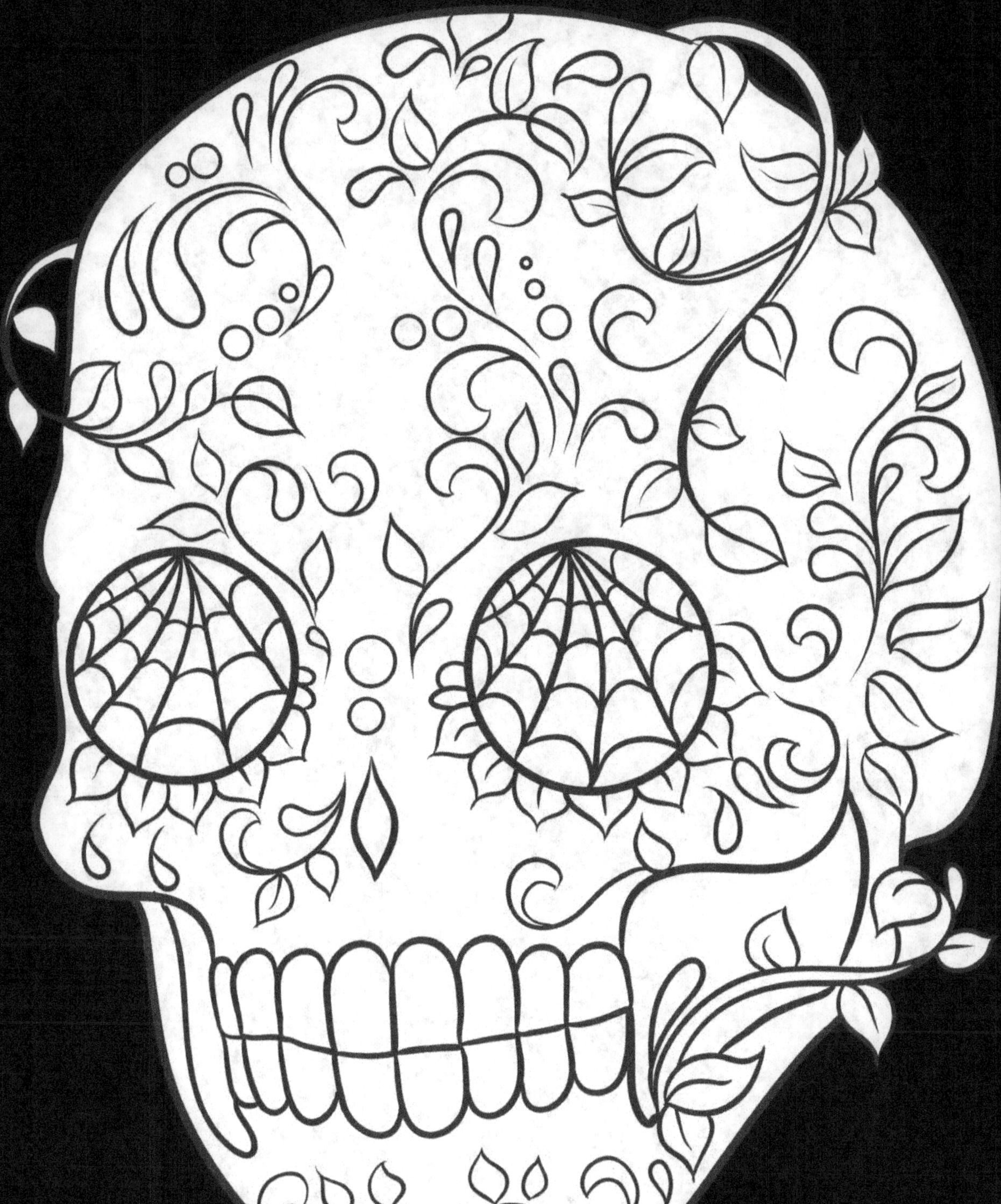

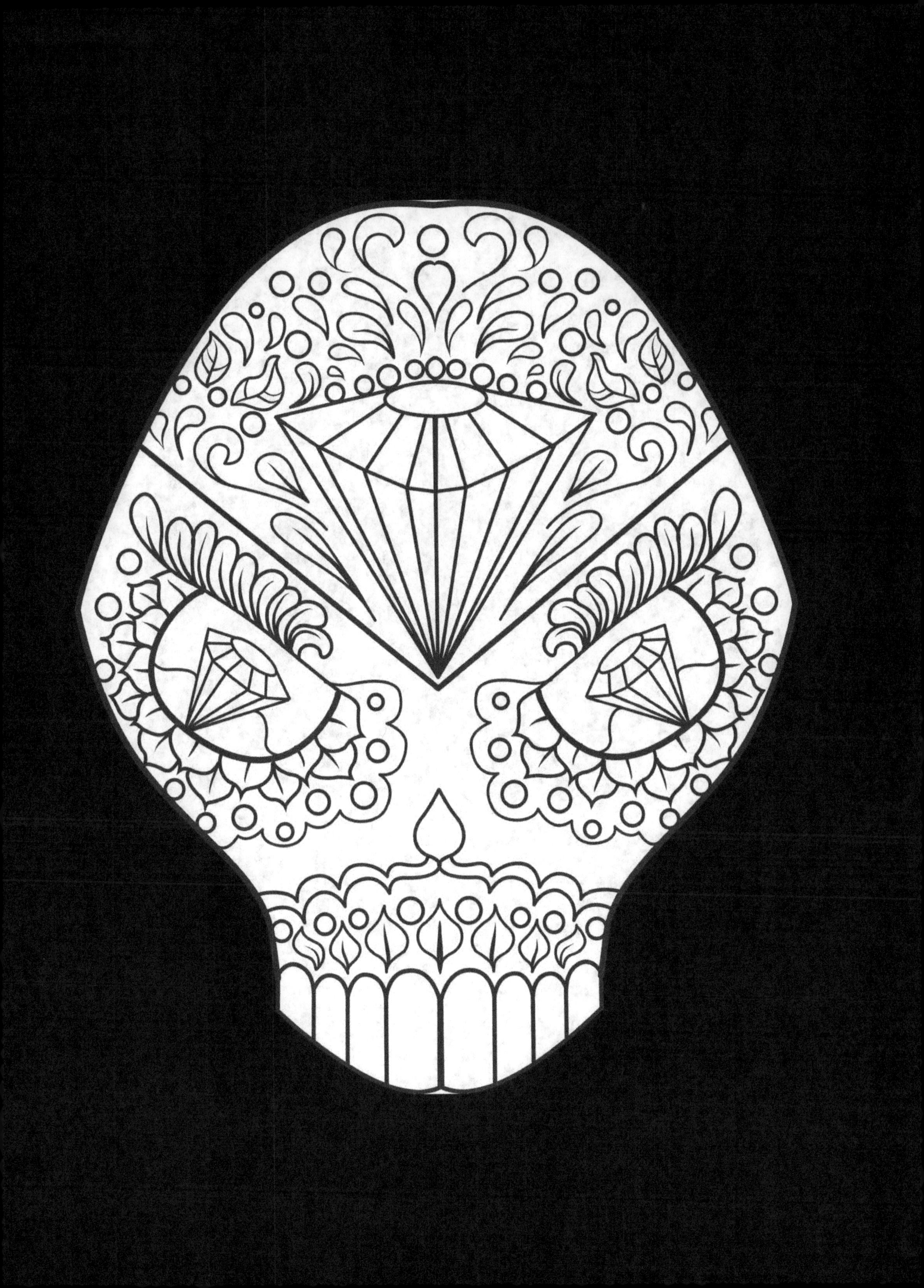

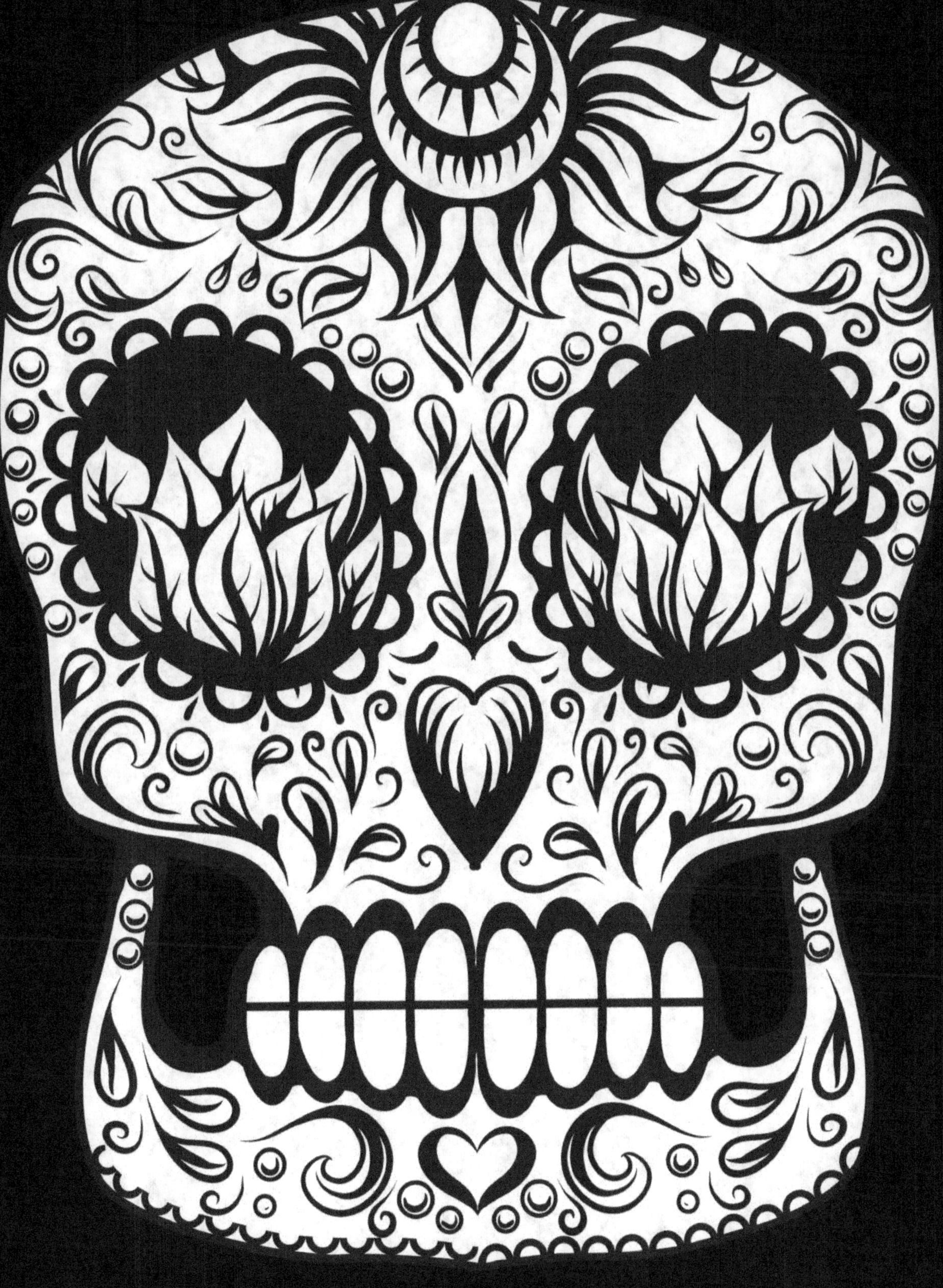

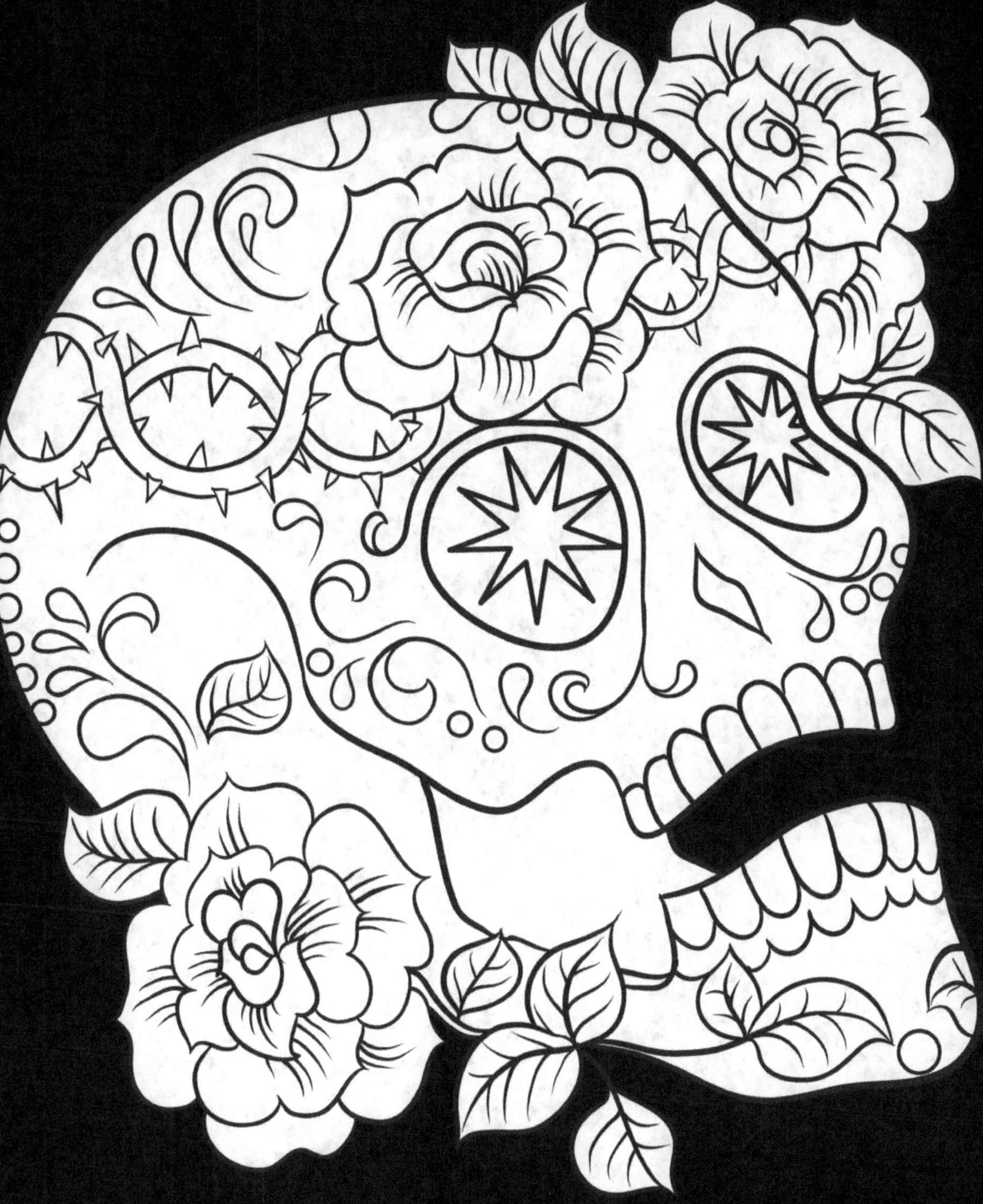

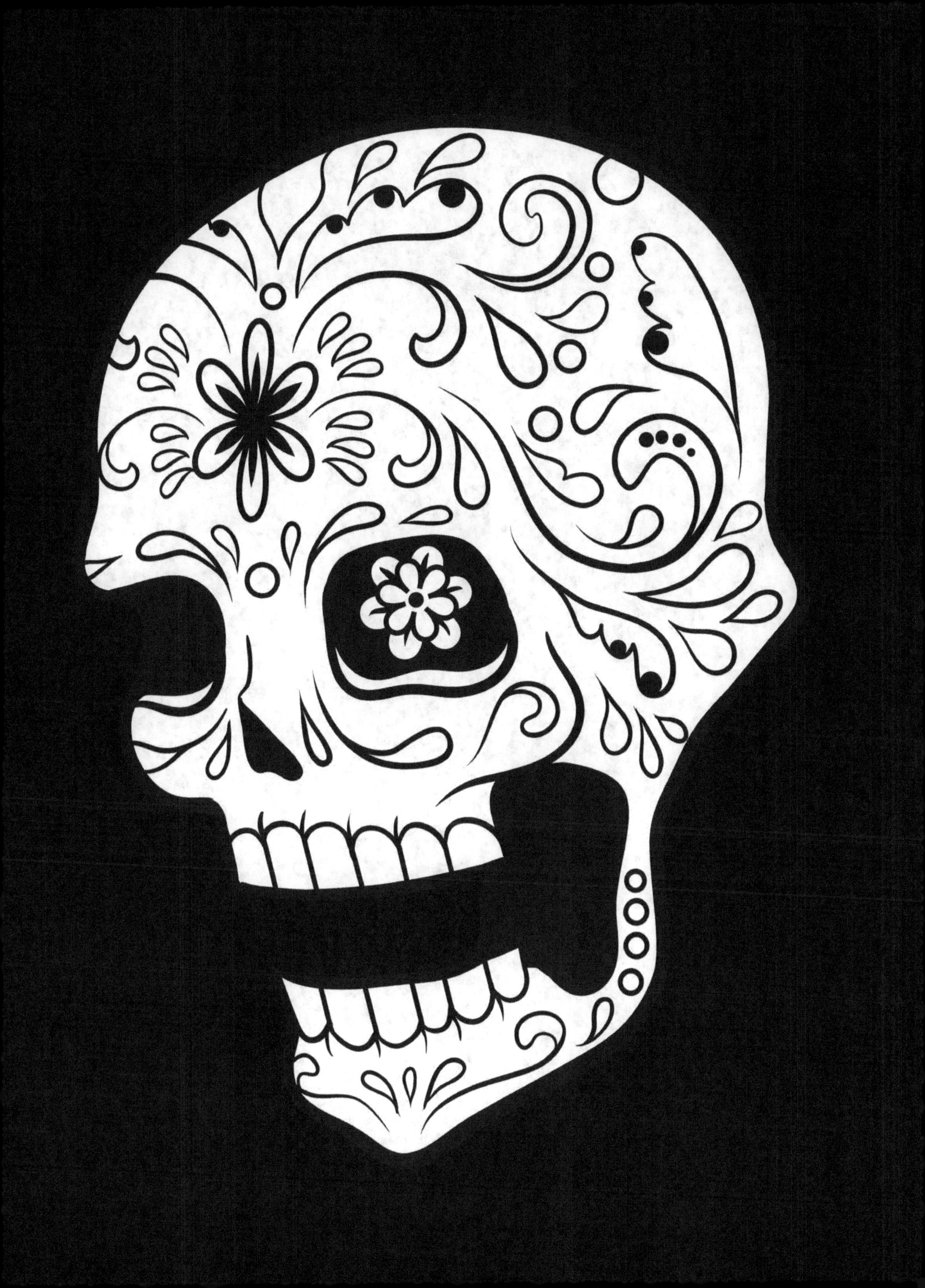

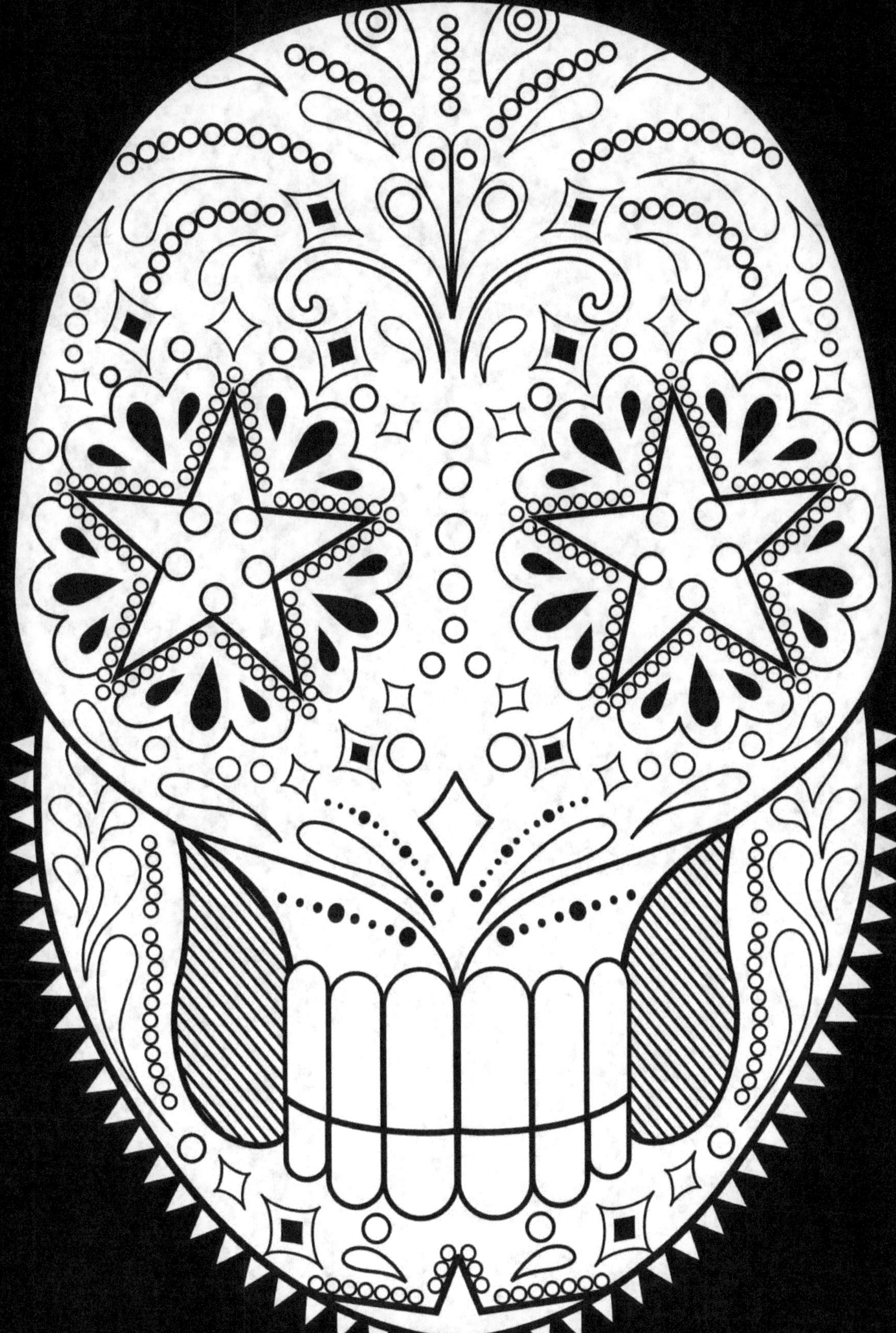

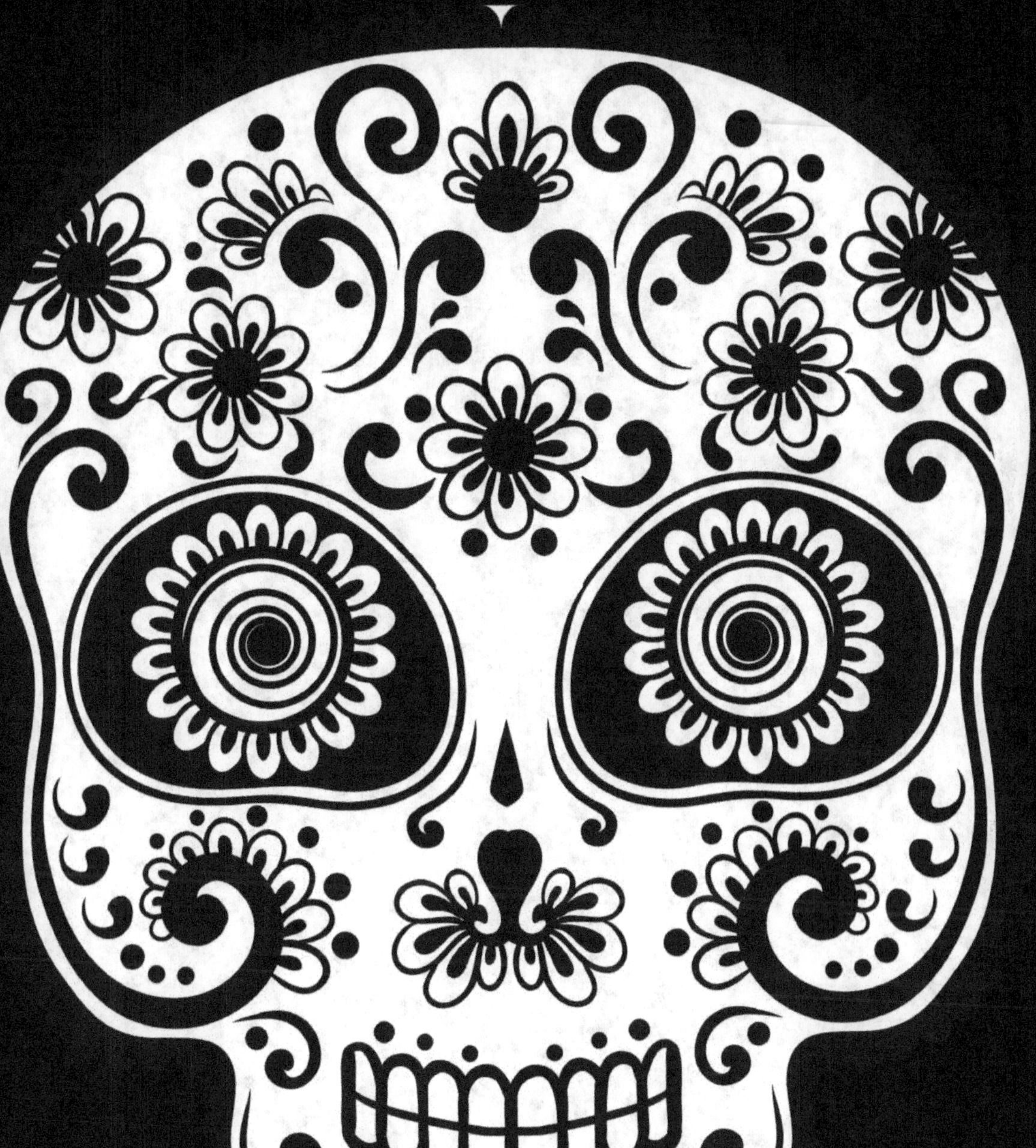

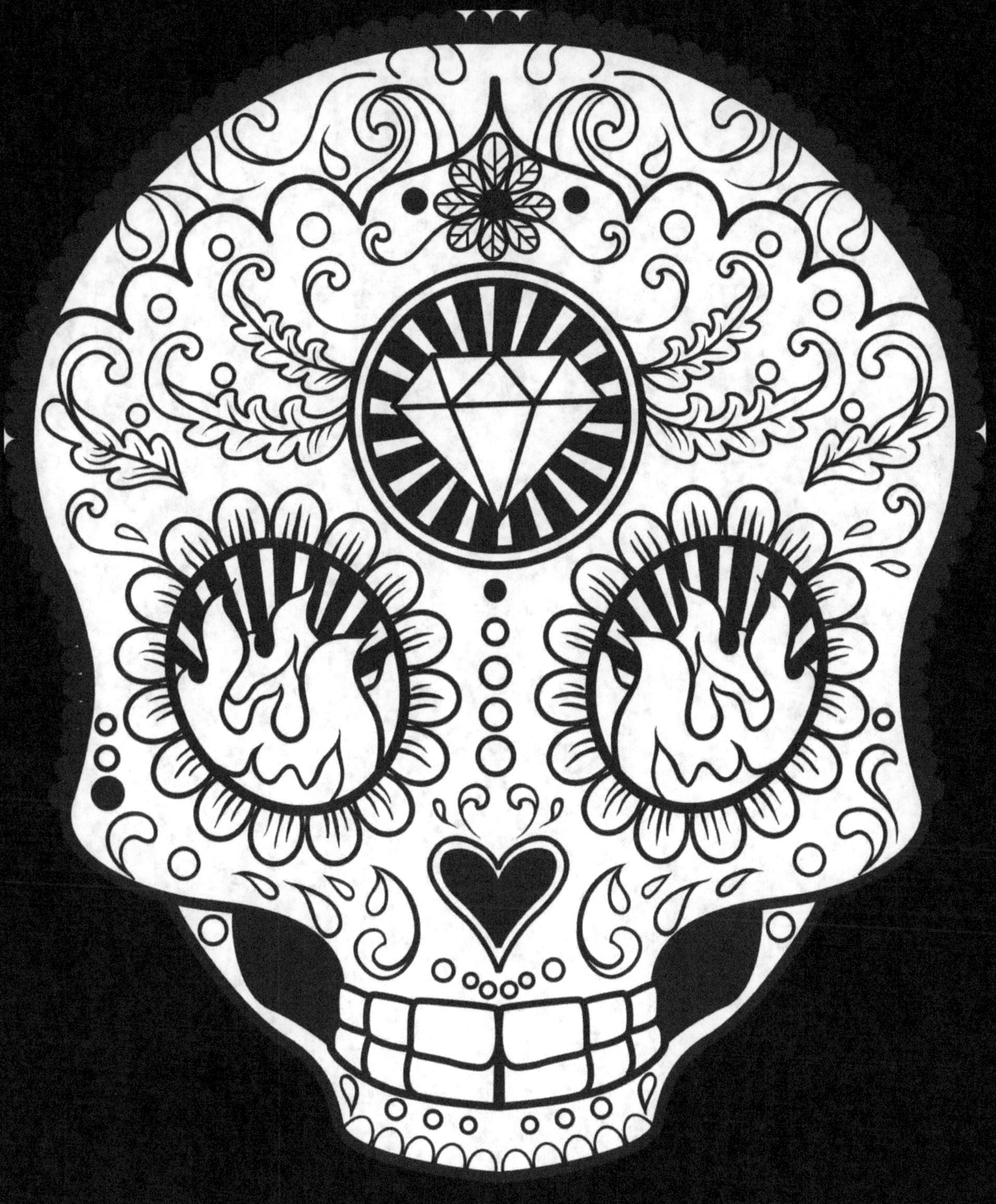

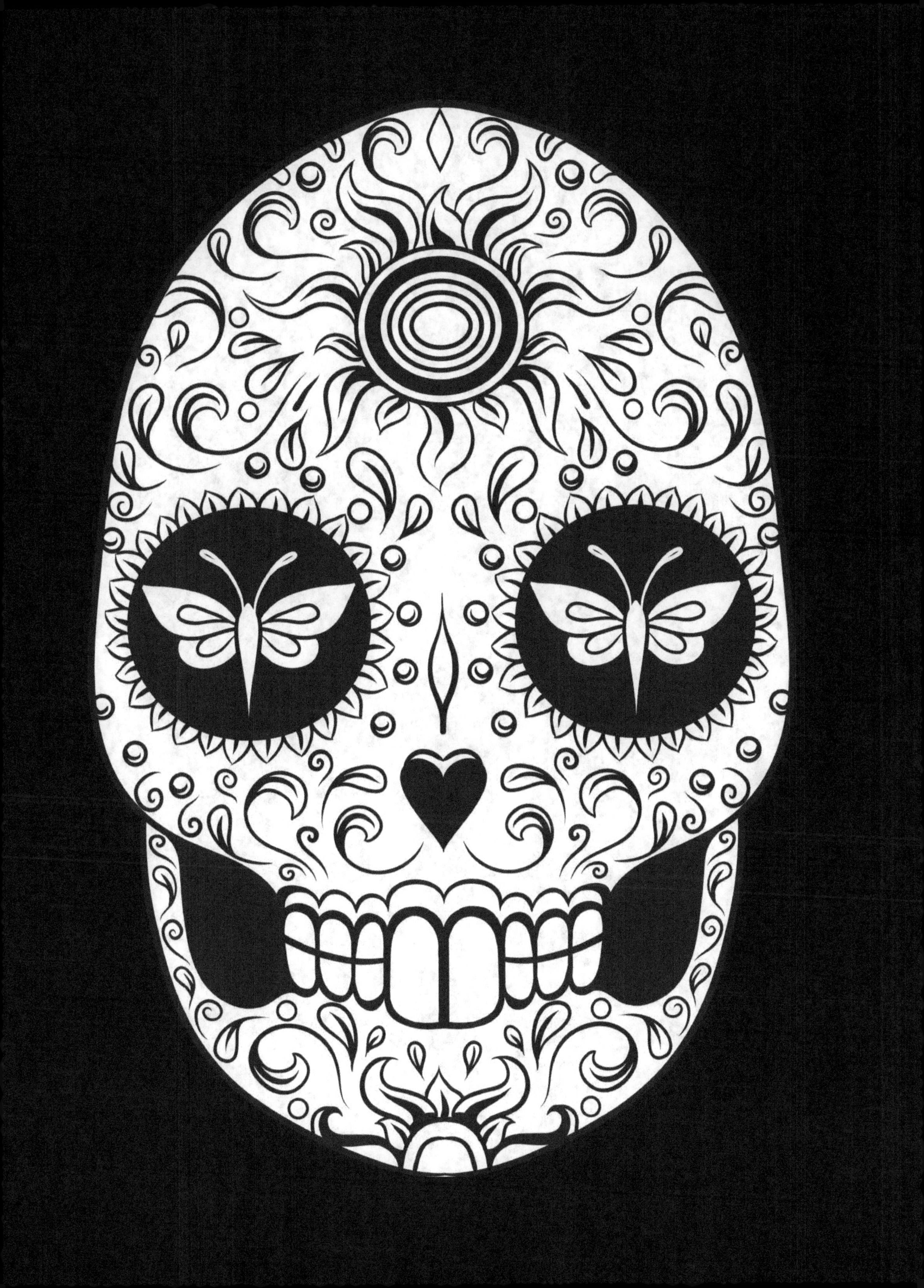

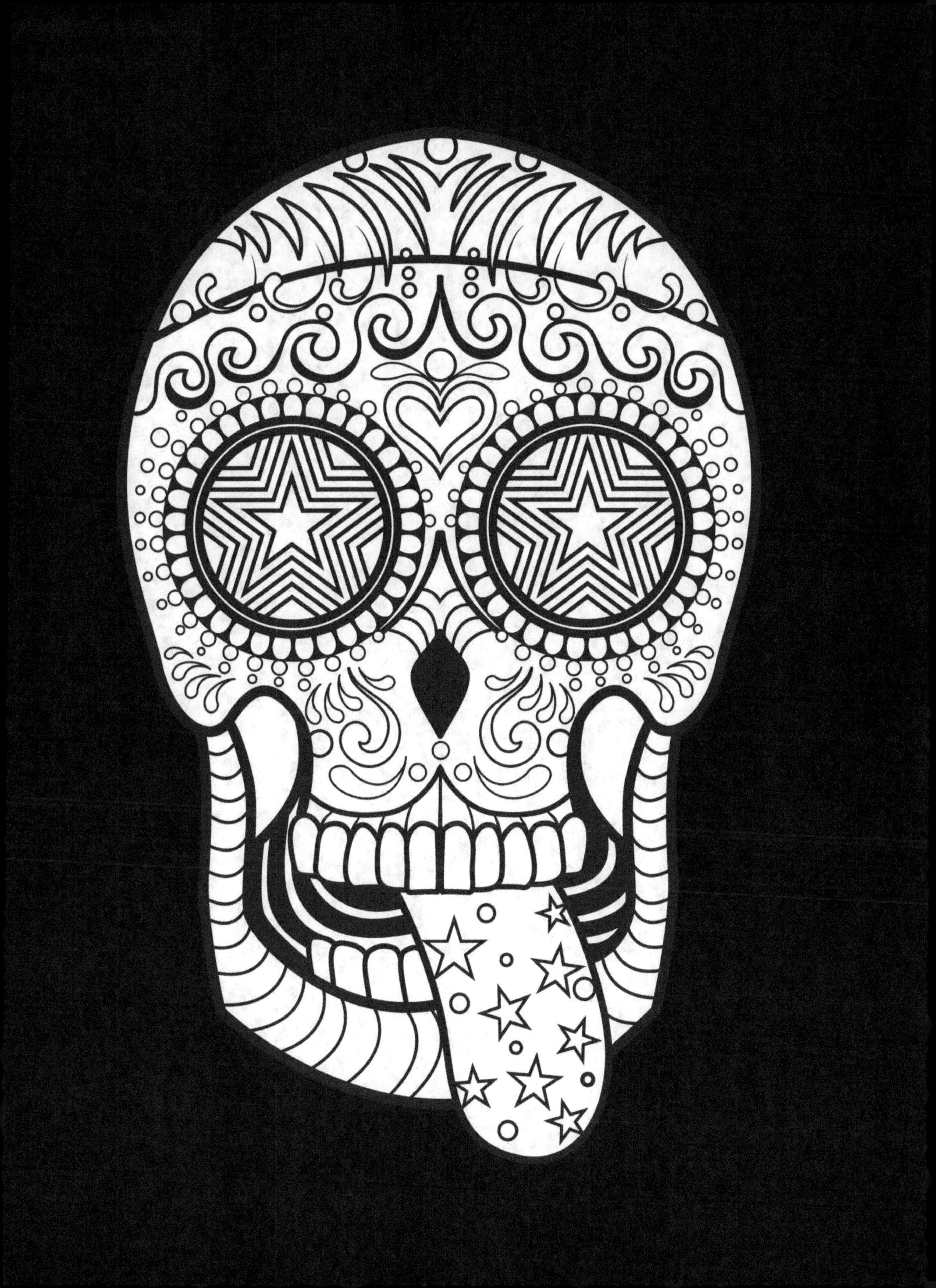

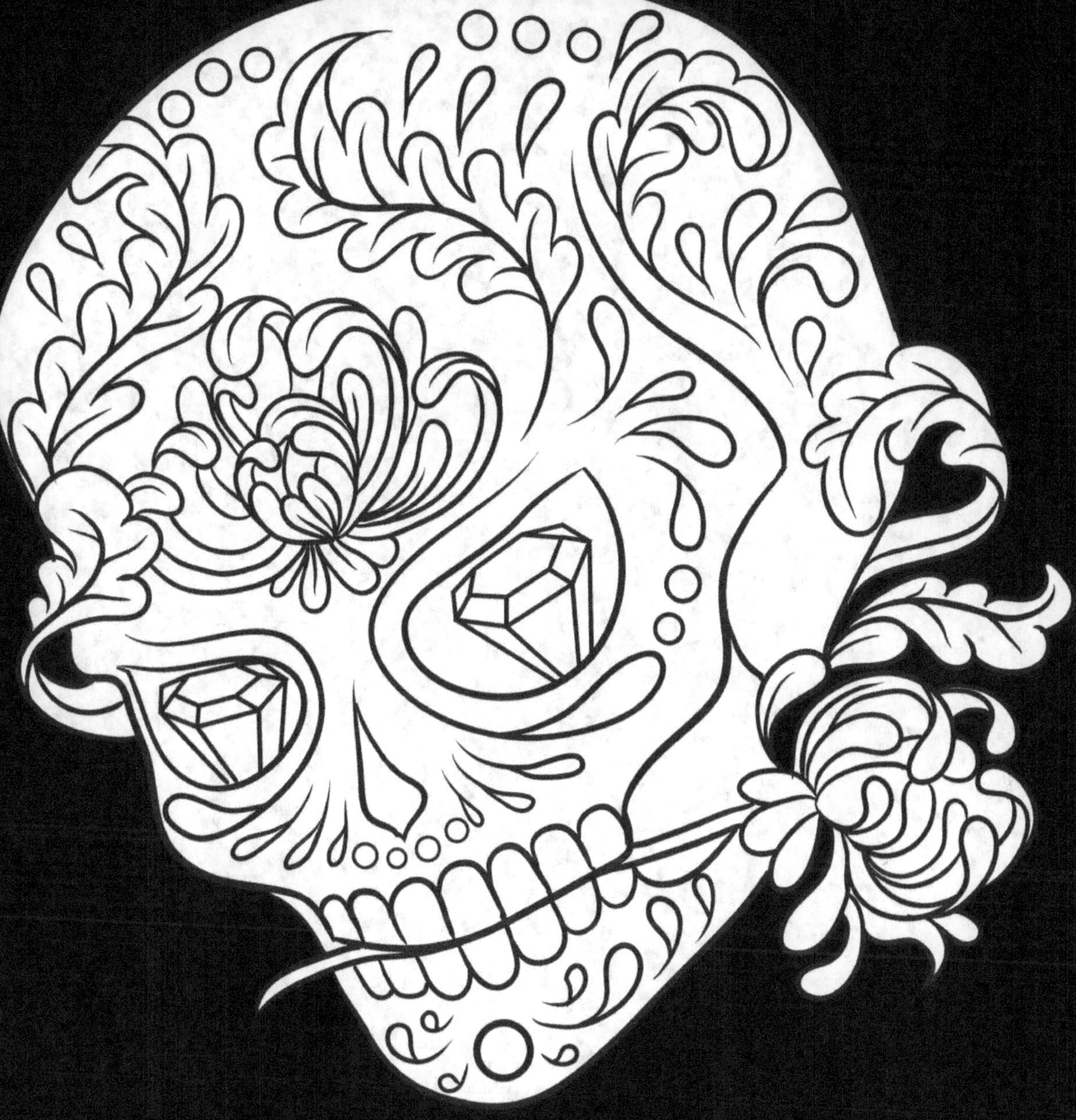

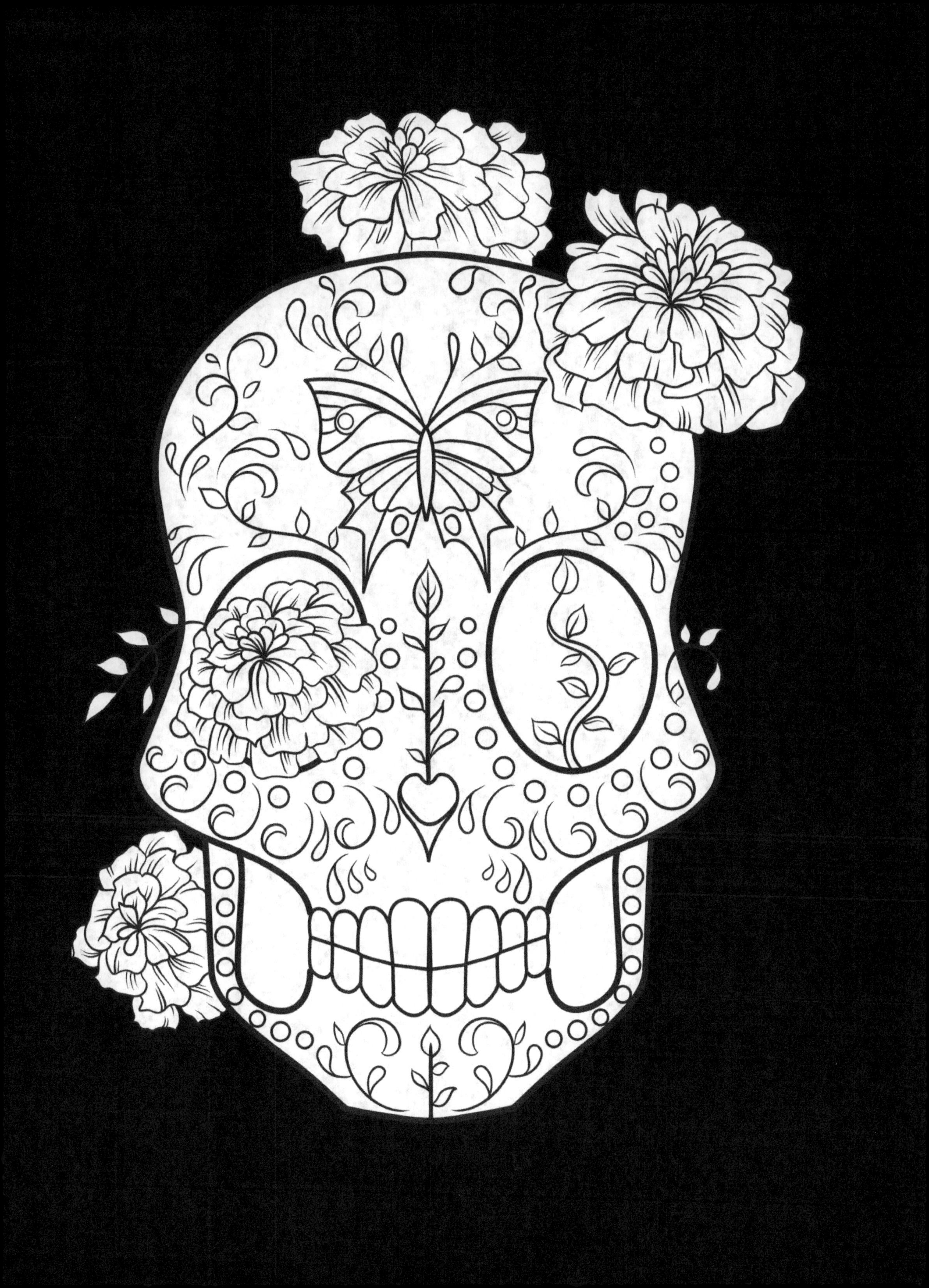

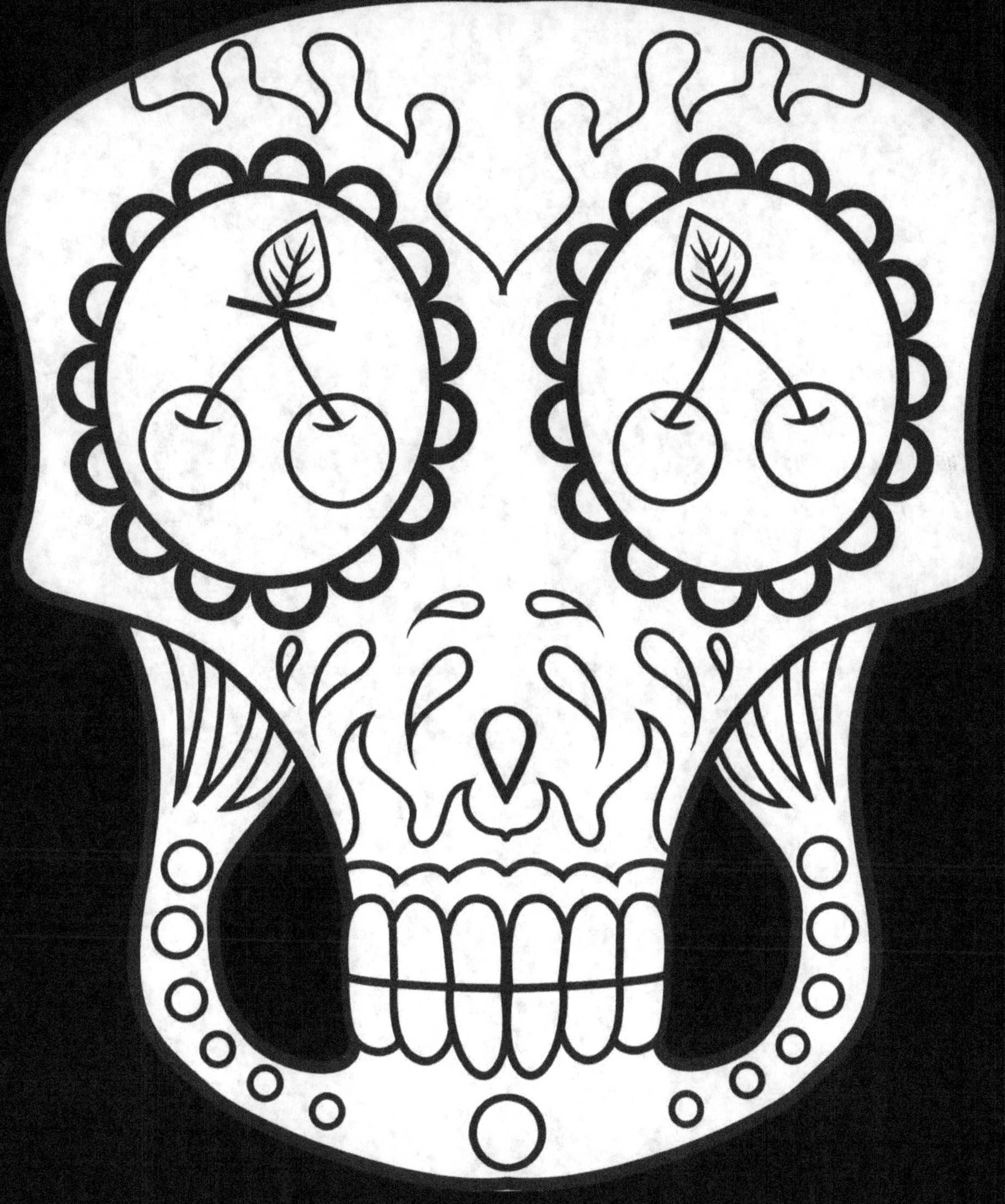

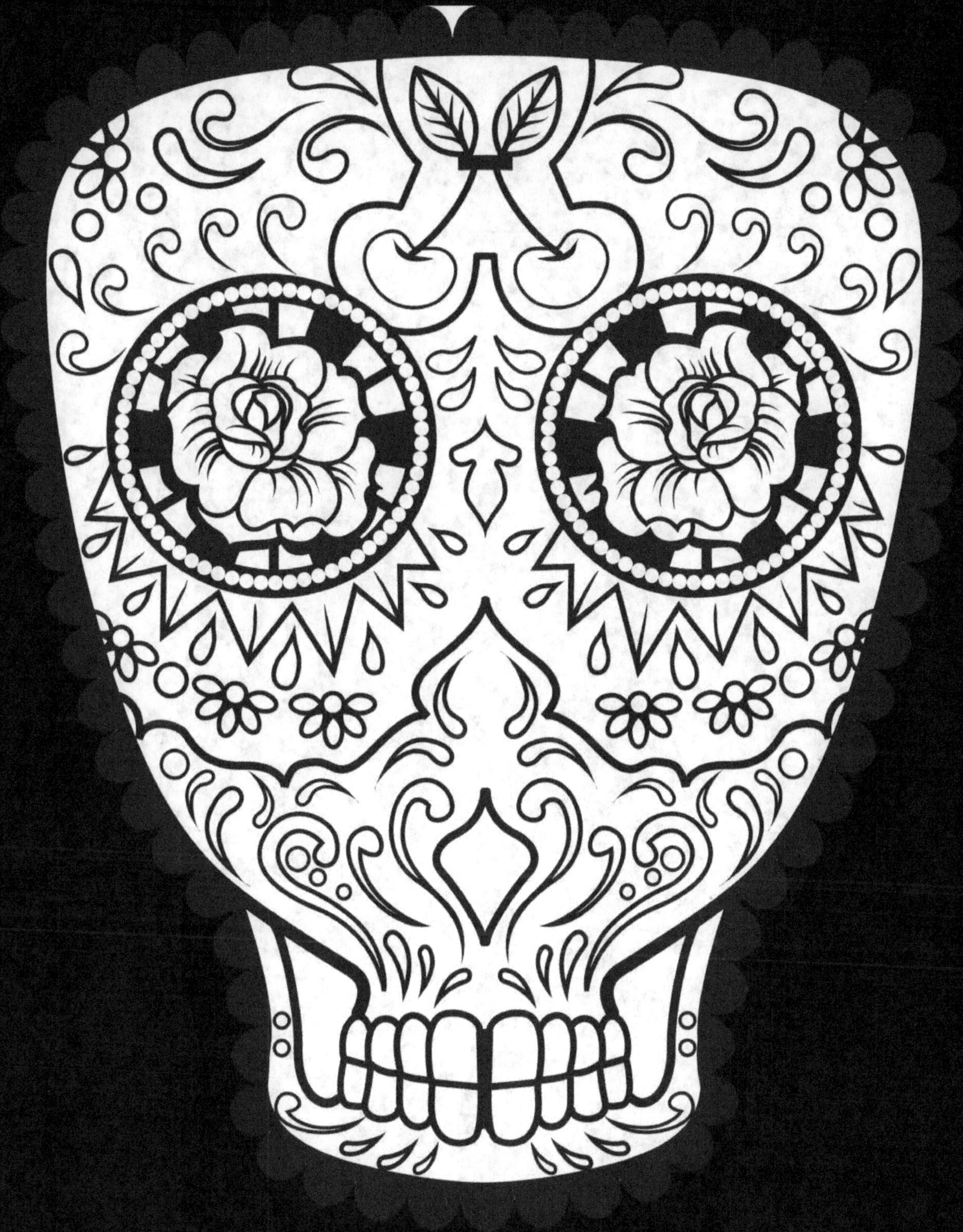

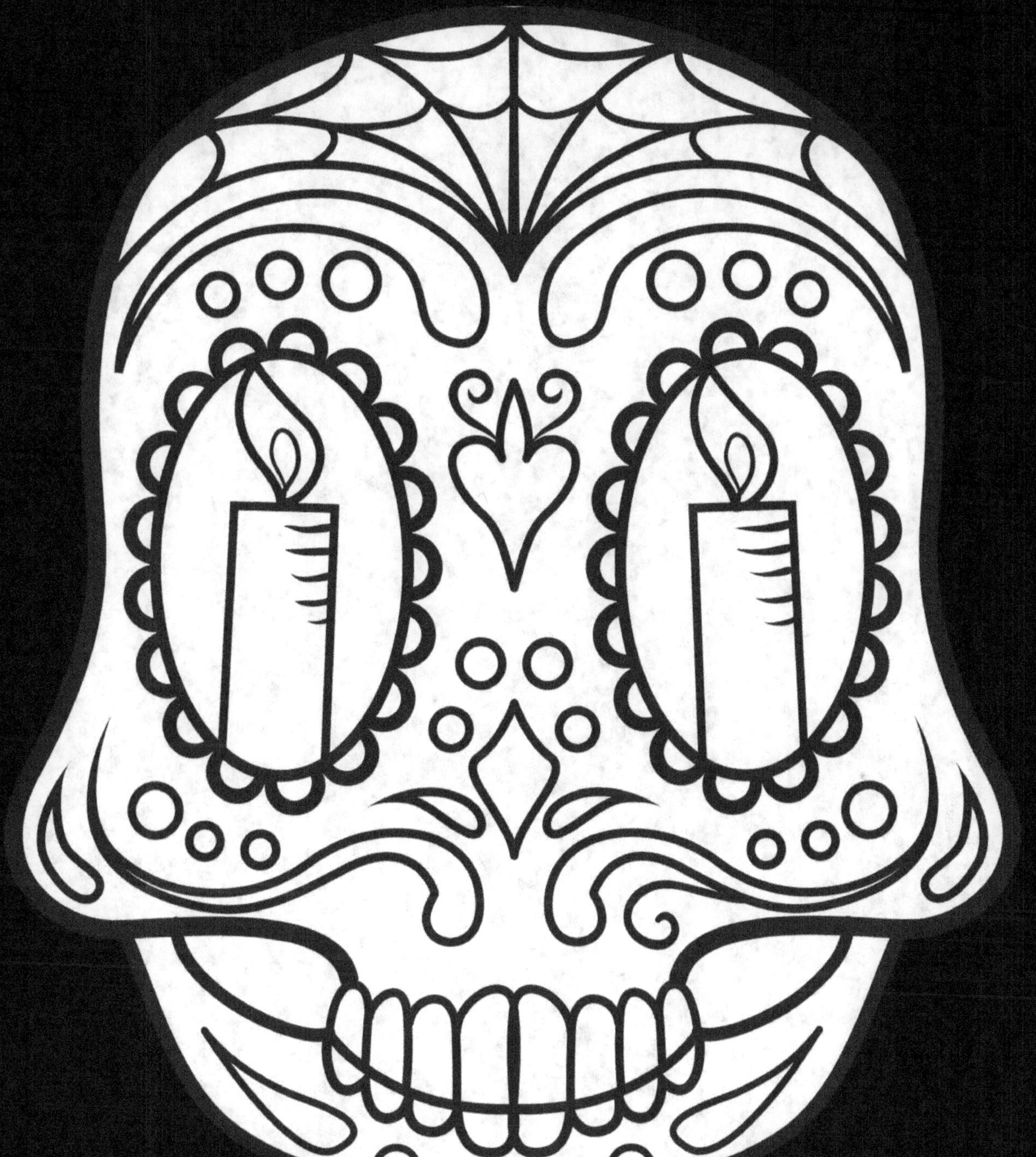

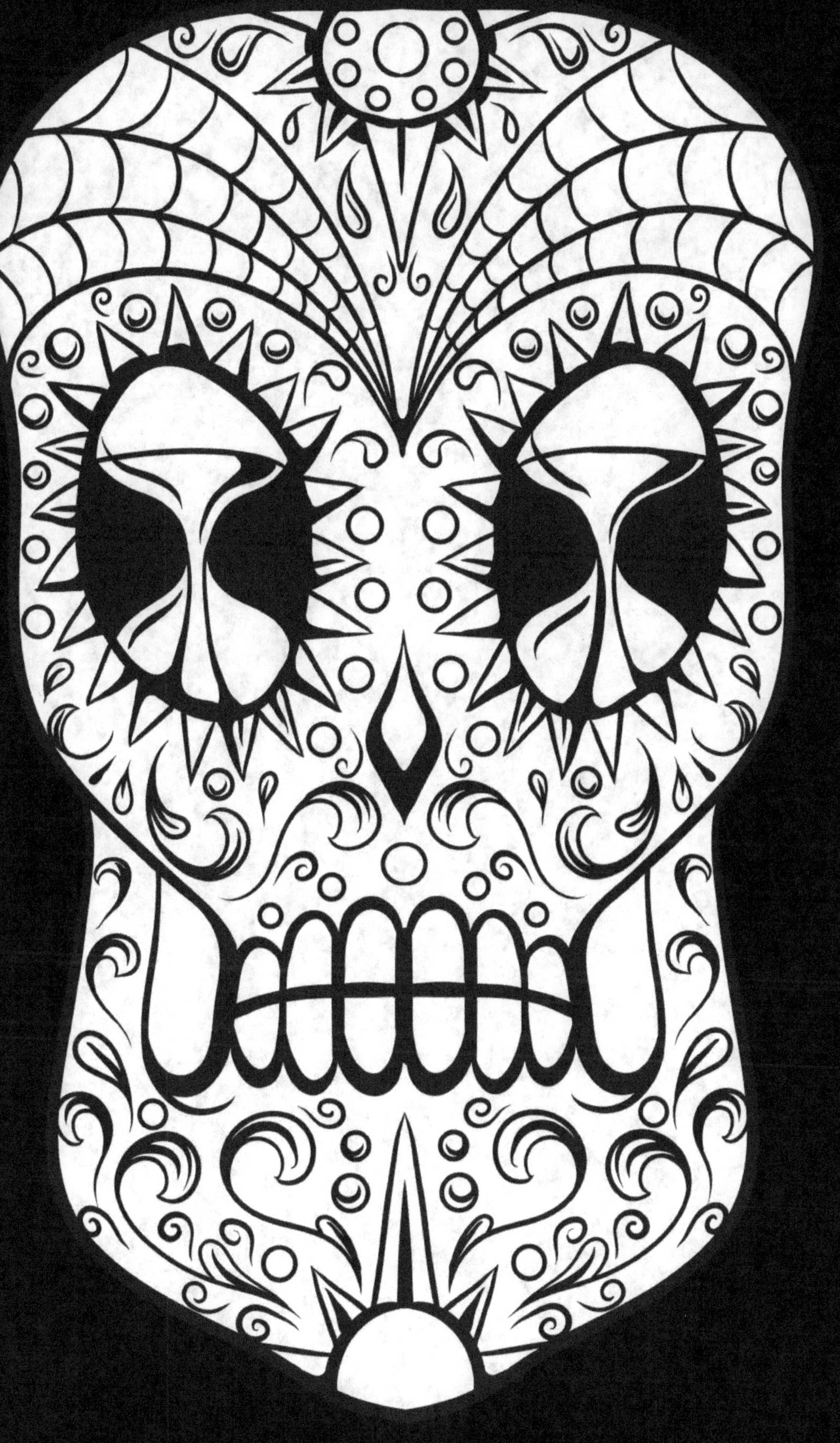

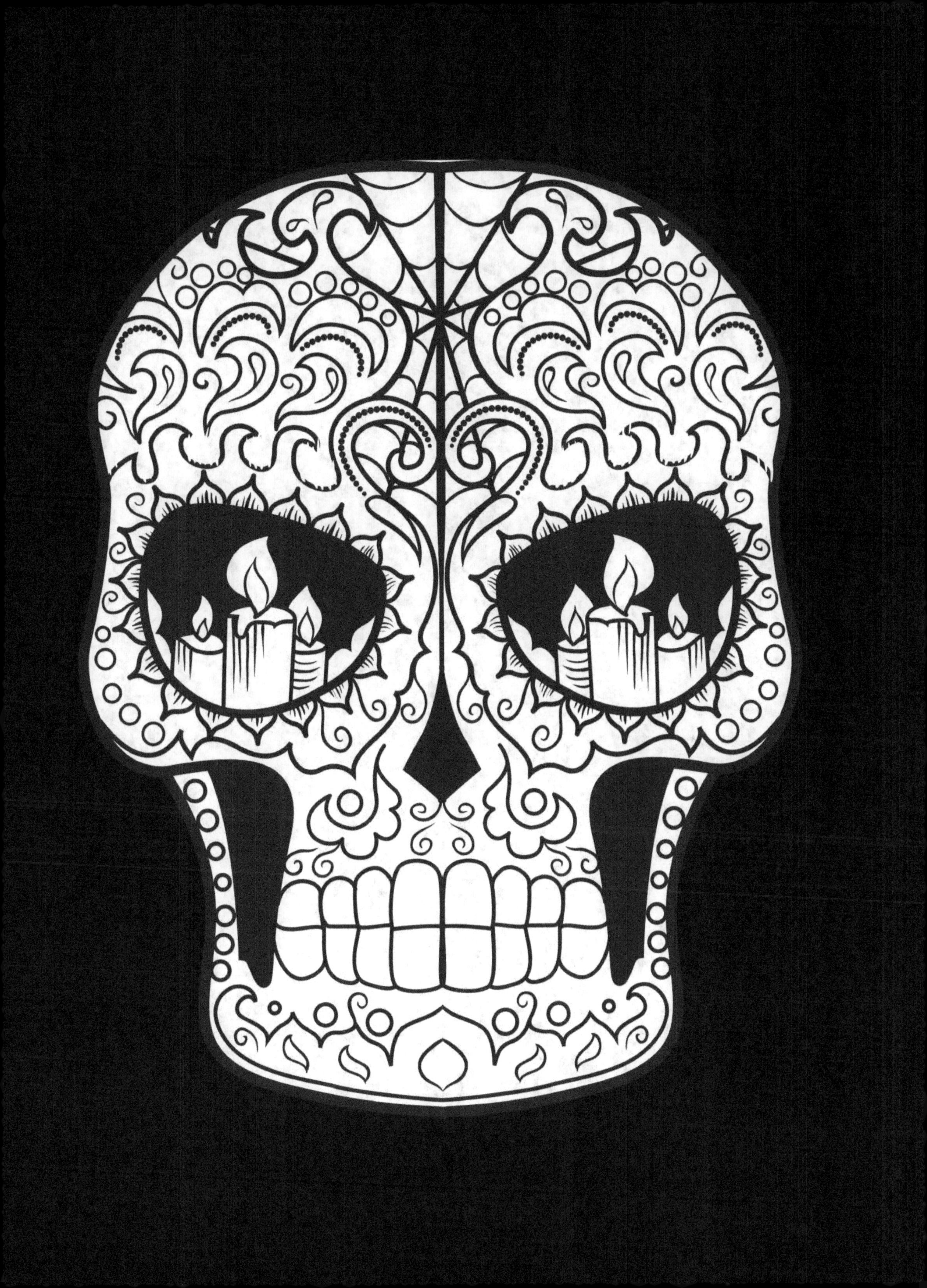

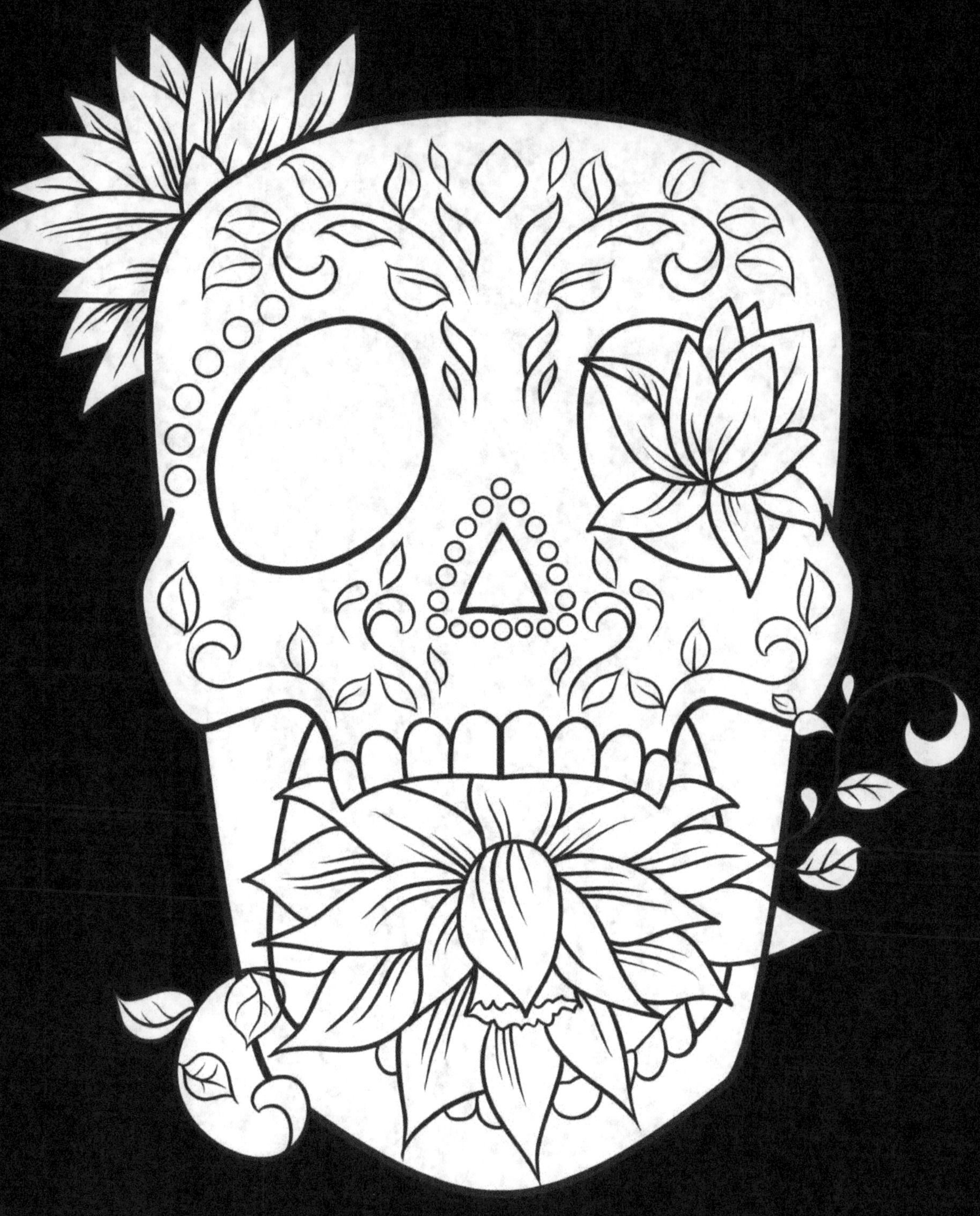

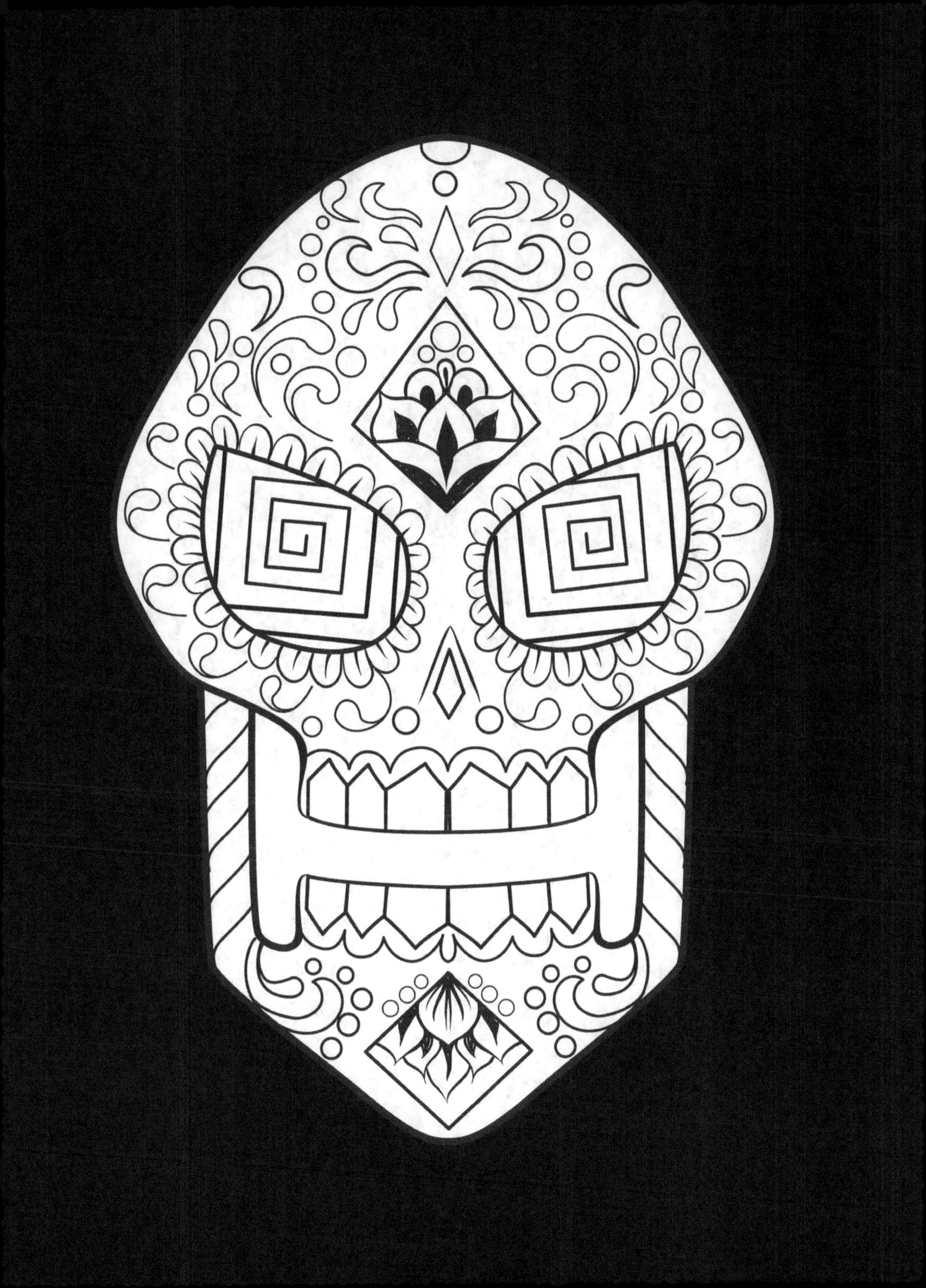

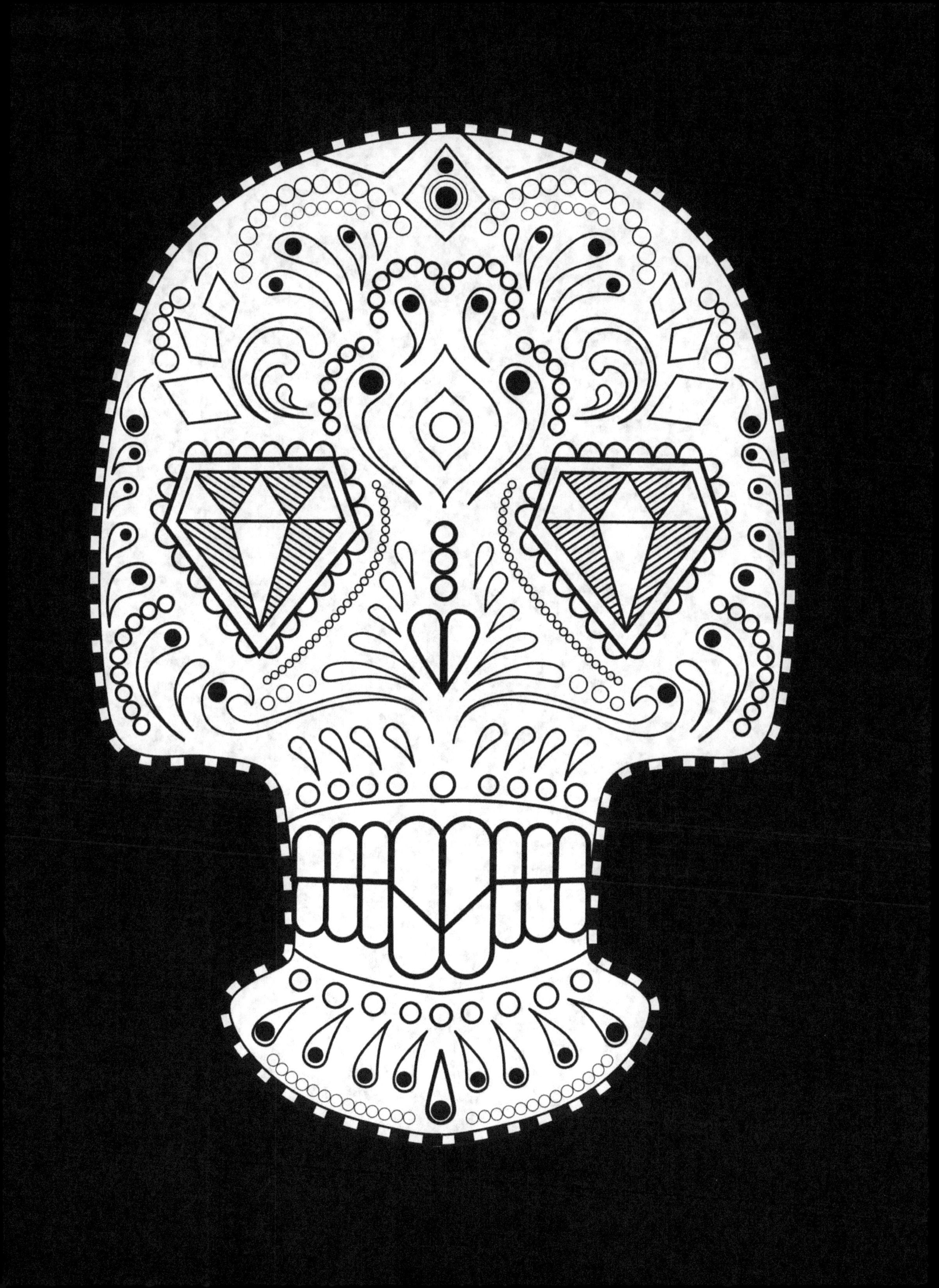

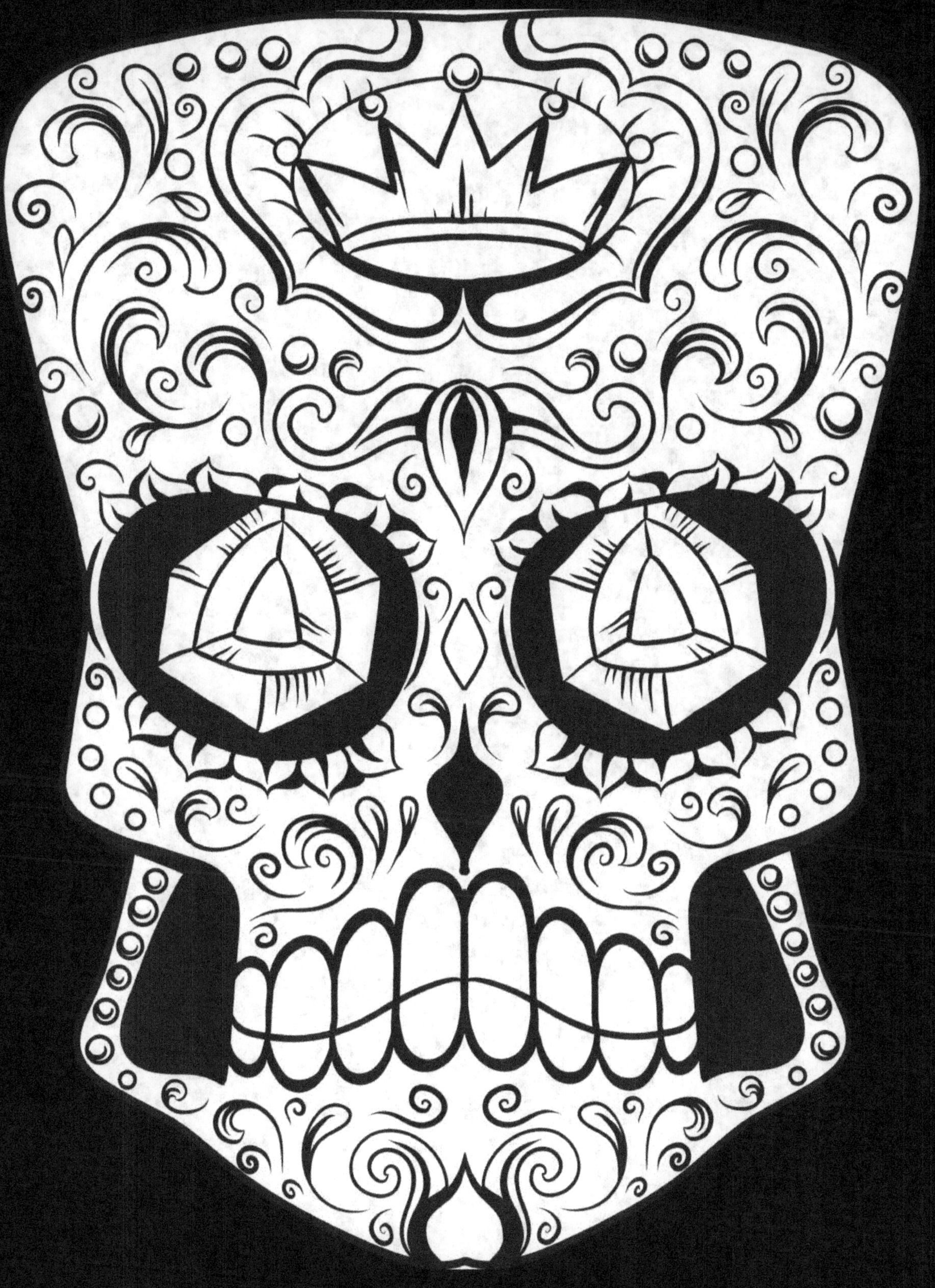

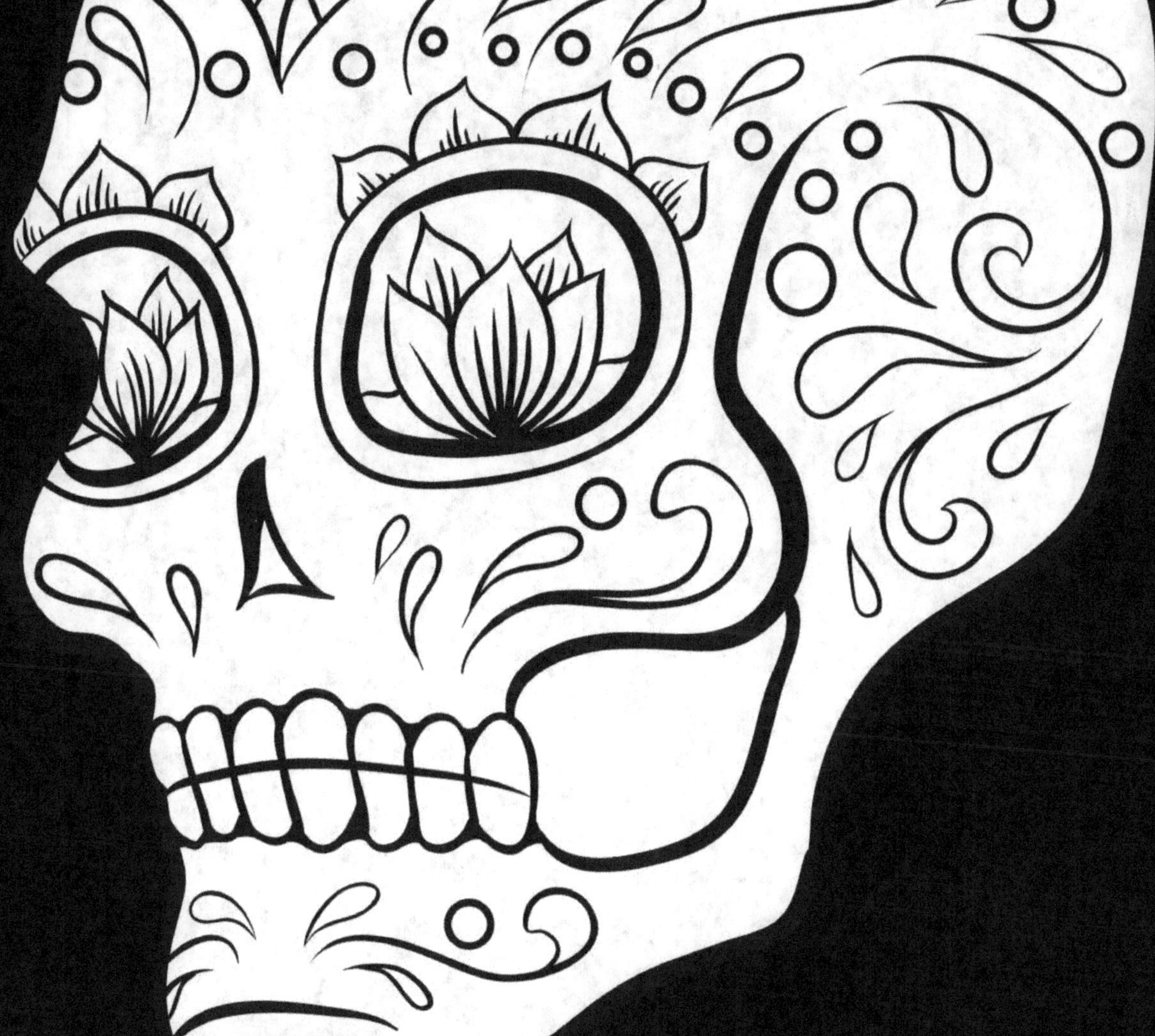

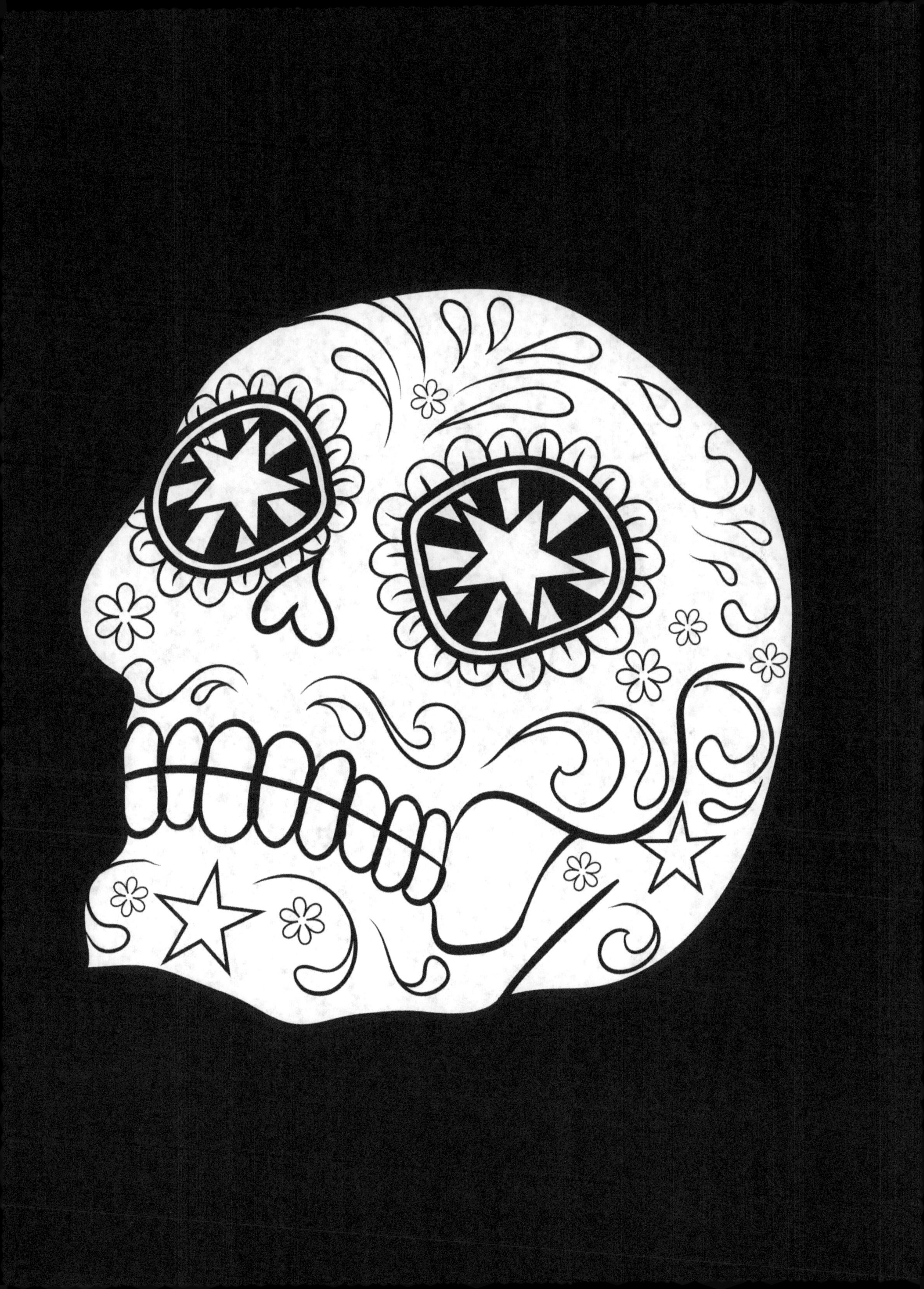

www.ingramcontent.com/pod-product-compliance
Lightning Source LLC
Chambersburg PA
CBHW082014290526
45787CB00016B/2808
9781534996663